The "Redlegs" of Barbados

The "Redlegs" of Barbados

Their Origins and History

by

Jill Sheppard

Foreword by Sir Philip Sherlock

The Caribbean—Historical and Cultural Perspectives
Robert Hill, *General Editor*

kto press

A U.S. DIVISION OF KRAUS-THOMSON ORGANIZATION LTD.
MILLWOOD, NEW YORK

Library of Congress Cataloging in Publication Data

Sheppard, Jill.
    The "Redlegs" of Barbados, their origins and history.

    (The Caribbean, historical and cultural perspectives)
    Bibliography: p. 139
    Includes index.
    1. Poor—Barbados. 2. Indentured servants—Barbados—History.
I. Title: II. Series.
HC157.B353P617   301.44'1   76-56886
ISBN 0-527-82230-2

First Printing 1977
Printed in the United States of America

Contents

Illustrations

Foreword

Names have a strangely terrifying power. Those who think in categories of magic, as Martin Buber points out in his study of Moses, have always known that the "true" name of a person is not a mere label but the very "essence of the person." A similar point is made by Harold R. Isaacs in *Idols of the Tribe* (New York: Harper and Row, 1975), where he reminds us that to be without a name "is almost not to be." He goes on to refer to the lexicon of epithets that members of different groups have for others: "The list in recent American English is familiar; nigger-coon-jig-wop-guinea-kike-yid-sheenie-mick-spick-chink-jap-honky-polack-wog-gook-dink-frog-limey-kraut, etc. ... an ever-changing index to the ways in which people despise one another." We can add to the list other epithets for the people of whom Jill Sheppard writes in this book: "backra Johnny," "poor backra," "ecky-becky," "Redshanks," "Redlegs." Even where the name is used in a self-derisory way, and spoken with a smile, it does not lose its poison; and it colours the way in which the men and women of the group are perceived by others, whether it be the author of *Antigua for the Antiguans* (1844) who found the "Redlegs" the "most truly wretched a class" she had ever seen in her travels, and one incurably idle; or whether it be the more perceptive Leigh Fermor who saw them as a kind of fossil-society, "ragged white men ... pale Nordic people," descendants of the followers of Monmouth whose history ended with their arrival in Barbados.

Jill Sheppard shows that the story runs otherwise. In this straightforward, clearly-written account of the origins and history of the "Redlegs" of Barbados she brings us face to face with a group of persons who have for too long been neglected or, at best, treated as a museum piece; and in the process of tracing their history she also removes some of that poison in their name. In concentrating her attention on the "Redlegs," she traces their origin to the ship that arrived in the island of Barbados in 1627 "freighted with men and women servants." These were free people who had sold themselves into bondage for a period of five or seven years in order eventually to acquire a piece of land and some money with which to make a life of their own. As the number of indentured servants increased the island gained a wide range of skills; for there were among them ropemakers, shoemakers, chandlers, serge-weavers, cloth workers and the like; and surely we find here evidence of the beginning of that transfer of craftsmanship from Western Europe that at a later date enriched Barbados with elegant furniture and glorious houses and churches of stone.

As the story unfolds, we witness the transformation of this originally voluntary movement of people searching for a better way of life into the vast uprooting of people from Western Europe, and a little later on, Africa, that were to provide cheap labour for the plantations of the New World. Jill Sheppard shows how the ranks of the poor whites were filled by Cromwell's military ravaging of Scotland and Ireland, the persecution of the Quakers, and the transportation of prisoners of war as well as convicts; a truly motley group. They did not know how to work, and only peopled the hospitals and cemeteries, save that the servants and poor whites of Barbados peopled some of the Windward Islands, Jamaica, and the Carolinas. For a brief moment, however, we can widen the perspective in time and space, and note how that ship of 1627, coming to anchor in Carlisle Bay with its load of white indentured servants, is linked with the ship that, in 1511, sailed into the harbour of Santo Domingo with the first cargo of Africans brought direct as slaves from West Africa to the Caribbean; with that ship whose name was not recorded that sailed into Virginia's Jamestown harbour in August 1619, a year before the Mayflower, and exchanged some African slaves for "victuals"; and with the Hesperus that sailed up the Demerara River in Guyana in 1838 and landed its cargo of one-hundred and fifty-six East Indian indentured labourers. Those who read the judgements passed on those East Indians and their descendants by the plantation society of the day will find them very similar to the judgements passed on the "Redlegs" of Barbados.

One of the many merits of this study is that is raises more questions than it answers. For example, we have so far given scant attention to the role of ideas and stereotypes in West Indian society. Dr. Elsa Goveia pointed the way in her brilliant book, *A Study of the Historiography of the British West Indies to the End of the Nineteenth Century* (Mexico: Instituto Panamerico de Geographia e Historia, 1956). Gordon Lewis developed the same theme in his book, *Puerto Rico: Freedom and Power in the Caribbean* (New York: Monthly Review Press, 1963). On a small scale we have here an illuminating example of the way in which white West Indian planter society saw itself and the world. All eyes are tribal, but some are more tribal than others, and when the planter looked at the slave he saw blackness as a badge of inferiority; when he looked at the white peasant he saw poverty as evidence of degradation. What Raynal said of the black slaves might have been said also of the white peasants: "We have almost persuaded them that they were a singular species, born only for dependence, for subjection, for labour, and for chastisement.

We have neglected these unfortunate people and we have afterwards upbraided them for their meanness." There is another question to be asked also, about the way in which the stereotype influences the self-concept of the individual and of his group. Is there not a strong case here for a programme of oral history that would involve the Barbados "Redlegs" and the poor whites of Mount Moritz in Grenada? Other questions raised have to do with the situation of a landless white peasantry in a slave society dependent on a black labour force, and with the relationships between the minority group of landless white peasants, and the majority group of landless black peasants after Emancipation.

West Indian society has been enriched by the work of many men and women who pursued their scholarly interests in such time as they had from their full-time occupation. Jill Sheppard has joined their company. I personally record my debt to her for the knowledge that I have gained from her book, as well as for the questions it raises. I hope that her history will find the many readers it deserves.

PHILIP SHERLOCK

Secretary-General of the Association of
Caribbean Universities and Research
Institutes; formerly Vice-Chancellor of
The University of the West Indies

Jamaica
July 1976

Acknowledgements

Many people have helped with the preparation of this book in a variety of ways and to all of them I am grateful; the omission of their names means only that I cannot include every one of them. I have, in the main, concentrated on those who have actually read the manuscript at various stages and provided comments.

Even as I write this I realise that I have to start with an exception to this rule: there were some people who provided most valuable assistance but did not get around to commenting on the manuscript. The suggestion that this book should be written in the first place came from Eric Armstrong, then Deputy Director of the Institute of Social and Economic Research at the Cave Hill campus of the University of the West Indies in Barbados, who some years before had collected a considerable amount of material on the subject of the poor whites of Barbados and who, since he had no time to continue with his study, most generously handed over all his notes to me. He thus provided not only the inspiration but also much of the background for this work, confounding totally those critics who allege a lack of generosity in academics.

Of my other colleagues at the University of the West Indies, Dr. Keith Hunte provided invaluable guidance at an early stage, as did also Dr. Roy Augier. Dr. Woodville Marshall and Tony Philips helped both with material and comments. Joycelin Massiah provided useful demographic material and advised on its use both in the text and in the form of tables.

To Sir Philip Sherlock, poet, historian, sometime Vice-Chancellor of the University of the West Indies, and now Secretary-General of the Association of Caribbean Universities and Research Institutes, I owe a particular debt of gratitude for his encouragement, his constructive comments, and the Foreword, which he somehow found time to do in the midst of his many other activities.

Other Caribbean scholars who provided both encouragement and comments—and at some stages the former was essential—include Professor

Gordon Lewis of the University of Puerto Rico, Professors Arnold Sio of Colgate University, Richard Dunn of the University of Pennsylvania, Connie Sutton of New York University, St. Clair Drake of Stanford University, and Professor Robert Rotberg of the Massachusetts Institute of Technology. If these learned professors find that their suggestions have not in all cases been adopted, they can nevertheless rest assured that they were much appreciated and very seriously considered.

One other exception to my rule is Professor Jerome S. Handler of the University of Southern Illinois. Not only was his *Guide to Source Materials for the Study of Barbados History 1627-1834* (Carbondale and Edwardsville: Southern Illinois University Press, 1971) a compendium of information, much of which I might not otherwise have been able to find, but he drew my attention to, and offered me the use of, the illustration of Sergeant Redshanks which appears in this book.

In Barbados the doyen of Barbadian historians, the Hon. H. A. Vaughan, drew on his vast fund of knowledge in commenting on my manuscript. I know that it does not quite measure up to his perfectionist requirements, but nevertheless I shall be happy if producing it in this form will enable somebody else to produce a better and more complete study. I am grateful also to Richard B. Moore, President of the Afro-American Institute, who commented in great detail on my first three chapters but who, I know, does not approve of my terminology.

Michael Chandler of the Barbados Department of Archives provided valuable help and comments on the manuscript; Edwin Ifill of the Reference Department of the Barbados Public Library and Ronnie Taylor of the Barbados Museum were a constant source of assistance with books and documents. The help provided by David Simpson of the Library of the Royal Commonwealth Society in London was most valuable, as was also that of the staffs of the British Museum and Public Record Office in London, and of the various libraries consulted in the United States of America.

I must also acknowledge my indebtedness to the Nuffield Foundation, which provided a grant which helped considerably in the production of this study, and to the Institute of Social and Economic Research of the University of the West Indies, and particularly to its then director, Alister McIntyre, which appointed me a Visiting Research Fellow and helped with a variety of matters, including the typing of the early drafts of the manuscript.

I should also acknowledge that a number of articles based on the information that I have acquired in the course of this study have appeared in *BIM*, the *Journal of the Barbados Museum and Historical Society*, the *Bajan*, the *West Indies Chronicle* and *Caribbean Studies*.

Finally, my thanks are due to Julian Marryshow, who read every chapter of the first draft of the manuscript as it came off the typewriter, and who was unreservedly critical of any lack of clarity both in the language and in the narrative.

Introduction

The memory of these things is lost in Barbados, where . . . no Barbadian knows why he calls another, or is styled himself a "Redleg"; a curious instance of the persistence of a name notwithstanding the loss of its significance.[1]

This was the view expressed in 1886 in Barbados, but the writer, a Chaplain at the Garrison, might just as well have been writing today. If he had done so, however, with the greater awareness at the present time of the emotive qualities of many of the words used to denote particular categories of people, he might have gone on to point out that the term "Redleg" has a distinctly pejorative flavour. He might also have noted that its use in Barbados is by no means consistent and depends to a large extent on the status and point of view of the speaker; while some prefer to use the term "poor whites" generally, others differentiate between "Redlegs" in the country districts and "poor whites" in the capital, Bridgetown, and many use the colloquial expressions "backra Johnnie," "poor backra" or even "ecky-becky."[2]

Nevertheless, in spite of the variations in its current usage, and changes in its connotation down the years as well as some obscurity about its precise origins, there is no doubt that the term has a meaning today: to misquote a famous historian, "You recognise a 'Redleg' when you see one." There is no question that the "Redlegs" have a distinct identity, belonging neither to the white 4 percent of the population, of which statistically they form a part, nor to the black 91 percent of the population, to the lowest echelons of which they are nearest in economic and class terms.[3] That this is not merely a figment of the imagination of travellers fascinated by "exotic" minorities was demonstrated in the early 1970s in a number of productions of entirely Barbadian origin.

In a programme of folk music from the eastern parish of St. John, where the last easily identifiable "Redlegs" are still to be found, a song entitled *Redlegs* was performed. This song, especially composed for the occasion but nevertheless in the folk tradition, in four brief verses and a refrain comprised references to several characteristic features of this particular subculture. It

1

included "Redlegs" as well as the other colloquial terms already noted; it
referred to favourite articles of diet, including coffee-tea, roast breadfruit and
red-crab sauce; it described the physical appearance of the people, with an
explanation of the term "Redleg" as deriving from:

> Yella hair, speckly face and dey feet brick red
> Is fo' dat we does call dem de Redlegs.[4]

Again, in an experimental musical play, *Unchained*, written and produced
by a group of young writers trying to find an indigenous performing art, the
first scenes depicted a group of tramps in Bridgetown, speaking and singing in
broadest Bajan dialect, and featuring prominently a "Red Man." This derelict
figure, wearing a dirty khaki shirt and trousers apparently cast off by a much
larger man, shambles and lurches about the stage, swigging rum and begging
cigarettes. He is an object of derision to his fellows, he is a joke figure, but he
is treated by them with good-natured humour. He is obviously by far the
most useless member of this company of tramps, yet he is picked up when he
falls and he will not, the audience feels, be allowed to starve. He is "one o'
we"; he is part of the group and in no sense an outsider. He is an individual
who eventually has a role, as is illustrated symbolically at the end of the
play, in a world free from prejudice and strife.[5]

A novel by Lionel Hutchinson, *One Touch of Nature*, studied in detail a
"Redleg" family against its background of a crowded lower-class area of
Bridgetown. The father of the family had come to town from the country
with no more than a shilling in his pocket and, while he cannot in any sense
be said to have made his fortune, he eventually achieves a steady job and
produces children, some of whom will become middle class. While life in the
cheek-by-jowl wooden houses of Lambert's Lane provides little opportunity
for exclusiveness on grounds of colour, the main character, Harriet, who
works in a big store as a shop assistant, or "clerkess," is plagued by considera-
tions of colour in her sex life. The novel ends with her impending marriage to
a black man, a civil servant. While she herself will never lose her conscious-
ness of being a "Redleg," her children will be both coloured and middle
class, and thus the stigma will have been removed.[6]

It seems a far cry from the sultry Lambert's Lane of Bridgetown, Barbados,
in the third quarter of the twentieth century to the bleak, windswept
highlands of Scotland in the middle of the seventeenth century whence the
origin of the term "Redleg" must be sought. The word "Redshank," defined as
"one who has red legs ... specially one of the Celtic inhabitants of the
Scottish Highlands and of Ireland," was in use at least from the sixteenth
century and continued in use until the nineteenth century, mainly with
reference to the Highlanders of Scotland with their bare legs and feet
reddened by exposure to the elements.[7] It is likely that the term first came to
Barbados with the Highlanders and other Scottish prisoners captured by
Cromwell in the late 1640s and early 1650s and then shipped to Barbados,

and possibly also with the Irish prisoners and deportees of the same period. It was no doubt perpetuated with the arrival in 1746 of the Highlanders taken prisoner at the battle of Culloden Moor. As an early twentieth century writer referring to the various influxes of people from the British Isles to Barbados describes them: "And lastly the Scots—the Redshanks whose name survives in the Redlegs (Poor Whites). Broken soldiers from Dunbar, Covenanters from the tolbooths of Edinburgh, Highlanders from Scotland they came, exiled 'from the lone shieling on the misty island.'"[8]

The explanation more usually provided of the indentured servants from Scotland wearing kilts in the fields and thus getting their legs sunburnt seems, therefore, to be rather less than the truth.[9] However, it may well provide a partial explanation of the gradual substitution of "Redlegs" for "Redshanks," leading to the eventual disappearance of the latter, and the extension of the use of "Redlegs" to refer to indentured servants generally, whether or not they came originally from Scotland or Ireland. For just as the sun would be no respecter of national origins when beating down on the bare-legged labourer in the fields, neither would the slave, when remarking on the curious phenomenon of the white man's skin turning red on exposure to the sun, differentiate between the labourers from England, Wales, Scotland and Ireland.

The first appearance in contemporary writing of the term "Redlegs" seems to have been in 1798 in an account by Dr. J. W. Williamson, M.D., Fellow of the Royal College of Physicians of Edinburgh, who, having previously served in Jamaica, visited Barbados on his return journey to England. He reported:

> A ridge of hills, in the adjacent country, about the middle of the island, is called Scotland, where a few of the descendants of a race of people, transported in the time of Cromwell, still live, called Redlegs. I saw some of them; tall, awkward made, and ill-looking fellows, much of a quadroon colour; unmeaning, yet vain of ancestry; as degenerate and useless a race as can be imagined.[10]

A subsequent reference to "Redshanks" is in *The Yarn of a Yankee Privateer*. The hero, after his capture at sea, was in Bridgetown on parole in 1813 on his way to imprisonment on Dartmoor, and described the local scene:

> Around this statue (Nelson) might be seen at all hours of the day, a congregation of idlers of all colours ... as I have observed, the love of idleness, was the predominant passion with all; from the most wealthy and exalted down to that lowest of all beings, the "redshanks." The latter were miserable and degraded white men who, priding themselves on their Caucasian origin, looked with contempt upon the African race, many of them vastly superior, in every respect. These "Redshanks" lived in huts like the negroes, somewhere in the

suburbs of the town, and were almost naked.[11]

The next references, chronologically, occurring in the works of two pairs of observers, one British and one American, who visited the West Indies shortly after Emancipation to report on the situation of the freed slaves, were also to "Redshanks."[12] Indeed, the term appears to have been in current use at this period. J. B. Colthurst, who spent the period from November 1835 to January 1838 in Barbados as a Special Magistrate, not only devoted several pages of his journal to describing the "Redshanks' of the Militia ("a most idle and good for nothing set—proud, lazy and consequently miserably poor") but also embellished his words with a water colour of "Sergeant Redshanks."[13]

After this date, however, commentators appear to have settled firmly for "Redlegs," sometimes with reference to their residence in the Scotland district, in accordance with Williamson's statement; sometimes with comments concerning their Scottish or Irish origins, appending occasionally suggested explanations of the term "Redleg." Dr. John Davy, Inspector General of Army Hospitals, who was in Barbados from 1845 to 1848, comments at length on the "poor whites, or 'Redlegs,' as they are contemptuously called from the red hue of their naked legs."[14] Governor Rawson uses "Redlegs" for the first time in an official document in 1871, when he refers to the "'Poor Whites' or in Scotland ... 'Redlegs.'"[15] N. Darnell Davis, whose reference to "Redlegs" is the only one quoted in the *Oxford English Dictionary*, describes them in 1887 as the "descendants of the old clansmen (who) form a peculiar people at the present time in Barbados."[16] Quintin Hogg, giving evidence before the West Indies Royal Commission in 1897, remarked:

> Then there are in Barbados ... a certain number, of so-called "mean whites"—"Redlegs", they call them. They are largely the failures of families who have now been in some cases over three centuries in the island, and so far from getting black they get bloodless in appearance and the sun has given to those parts of the body exposed to it a colour which finds its expression in the local name of "Redlegs." ... It is a most pitiable thing to see them wandering about with some of the conceit of the white blood, but none of the energy of the European.[17]

Hence, in the earlier part of the twentieth century comments employing the term "Redlegs" abound. Perhaps the best known were those made by the travel writer, Patrick Leigh Fermor:

> We passed through the more hilly districts of Scotland, and observed, working in the fields or sitting in the doorways of miserable wooden shacks, not the Negro figures to which the eye is accustomed in such settings in the West Indies, but

ragged white men with blue eyes and tow-coloured hair bleached by the sun. This little population of Redlegs, as they are called, are descendants of the followers of the Duke of Monmouth, who, after their defeat at Sedgemoor, were deported by order of Judge Jeffries at the Bloody Assizes. They have remained here ever since, in the same humble plight as when they were first herded ashore.[18]

This particular Monmouth myth has been perpetuated by Nicholas Monsarrat who visited Barbados in 1956. After encountering some poverty-stricken white people somewhere in the "interior" of the island, whom he describes as "pinkish, and shambling, and odd," he claimed to have been reminded of a family of fishermen of similar appearance he had once come across in the Eastern Province of South Africa. Intrigued, he does what he refers to as "a small piece of research" and produces the theory, which he refers to as the "truth," that these "Redlegs" are the direct and only descendants of those Monmouth rebels who, escaping the hangman's noose, were sentenced to transportation to Barbados.[19]

The impression conveyed by this handful of extracts, chosen primarily for their usage of the terms which have variously been employed, suggests that there is still some obscurity surrounding the derivation and use of the term "Redleg," though it is not as complete as some writers have assumed. It also suggests that there is a considerable tendency on the part of observers to make comments of a highly subjective nature, which sometimes reach an almost inconceivable naivety—as is evidenced by the statement of Quintin Hogg. There also appears to have been abysmal ignorance about the social and historical background of the "Redlegs," if Patrick Leigh Fermor's and Nicholas Monsarrat's suggestions that the "Redlegs" of today are all descended from the Monmouth rebels are any criteria.

In truth, however, the history of the "Redlegs" commenced with the arrival in Barbados of the English settlers in February 1627, who brought with them their white servants who, by the time the slaves started arriving from Africa, were generally designated as Christian Servants. It continued with the various waves of white immigrants, both voluntary and forced, who came flooding into Barbados in the middle years of the seventeenth century, and sporadically on into the next, to work on the plantations as indentured servants. Once their periods of indenture were over, those who did not emigrate, or in some cases better their positions, gradually formed a separate group within the white population. These people were known in the seventeenth century as freemen. As a writer late in that century points out, there were at that time four quite distinct classes of people: freeholders, owning at least ten acres of land, who have the right to choose the members of the assembly; "freemen, who, having served out their time of indenture are freed from their masters and serve for wages; servants, whose time had not expired; and negro slaves."[20] For most of the eighteenth century and later, they were generally designated, both in official documents and elsewhere, as poor whites. During the nineteenth century this term was still current and, while it had no legal definition, there is no doubt that it was used to refer to a class comprising all those white groupings outside the pale of the plantocracy and the closely allied business and professional classes, who, until the lowering of the franchise requirements in 1840 following Emancipation, had no vote since they possessed neither ten acres of land nor house property of the stipulated value.[21] It was during this period that the term "Redlegs" came sporadically into use, as was reflected in the main by observers from abroad.

The picture inevitably becomes obscured during the course of years. Just as there was some upward mobility so there was also the reverse, and some poor whites may have been the descendants of members of the planter class who had fallen on hard times. Nevertheless, there is no doubt that the poor whites formed a distinct class in the society, described as such in the Poor Relief Report of 1878 and defined there as comprising in the main the descendants of political deportees.[22] The history of this class is therefore examined in some detail through its two centuries or so of degeneration to its rehabilitation dating from the last years of the nineteenth century and extending through the twentieth century to the present day.

In the process of telling this story an attempt will be made to analyse the reasons for the degeneration of the indentured servants, the first of whom had made an essential contribution as agricultural labourers and artisans to the permanent settlement of Barbados, into a class of virtual "drop-outs." The repercussions for the indentured servants of the introduction of the slaves onto the plantation, later for the "freemen" of the increased use of slaves in skilled jobs on the plantations, and later still for the poor whites of the energy and drive of the free coloureds will be examined, as will also the effects of Emancipation, and particularly of the subsequent reorganisation of the Militia, on this class. The measures which were eventually to result in their rehabilitation will also be discussed.

Throughout the study the terms used will be the ones appropriate to the period. Hence the use of the appellations "Redlegs," poor whites, freemen, indentured servants, and Christian servants, back to the servants of those first settlers with whom the story opens.

The Indentured Servants

Chapter 1
Settlement (1627–1642)

The first group of English settlers who arrived in Barbados in February 1627[1] included not only gentlemen, no doubt some of them impoverished, seeking their fortunes, but also a proportion of servants, to whom fell the hard physical work involved in trying to create a plantation out of a wilderness. For, in spite of the fact that the English were by no means the first people to inhabit the island, or, indeed, the first Europeans to set foot there, Barbados was at that time uninhabited and showed no immediately obvious traces of any type of habitation or cultivation. Archaeological and other evidence indicates, however, that the Arawaks, coming from South America into the Caribbean, had a stable agricultural and fishing industry on the island for some centuries until early in the sixteenth century, when they disappeared for reasons which have not yet been satisfactorily established. Since the time of their disappearance, although probably visited by Caribs on fishing and hunting expeditions from neighbouring islands, and certainly by the Spaniards in the early sixteenth century and by the Portuguese, who left hogs there to provide food on future visits, there do not appear to have been any permanent residents in Barbados for just over a century.[2]

This lack of habitation was obviously an important factor in encouraging Sir William Courteen, a rich merchant controlling an important trading company operating in England and the Netherlands, to establish a permanent settlement on the island. A claim had been staked in 1625[3] by John Powell when he disembarked at a point on the west coast, now called Holetown, and who made it clear that he was annexing the island for the King of England when he set up a cross and "inscribed on a Tree adjoyning James K. of E. and this Island."[4] On his return he reported to Courteen, his employer, who immediately fitted out an expedition under the command of John's brother, Captain Henry Powell, to travel to the island and start planting operations.

Powell and his ship *William and Mary* reached Barbados in February 1627. The island on first sight, with its dense forests, thickets and shrubs extending

7

down to the shore, must have presented a daunting picture to that first shipload of men, exhausted as they would have been after two to three months of inadequate food, cramped conditions and the inevitable fear of shipwreck or enemy attack while crossing the Atlantic. Naturally, their first requirement was to erect makeshift shelters to protect them not only from the elements but also from the various unfamiliar forms of insect and animal life, and to find food to eke out and supplement whatever stores remained after the voyage.[5] A contemporary writer refers particularly to their problem of supplies—"in such misery they have endured, in regard of their weakness at their landing, and long stay without supplies."[6] This no doubt caused Captain Henry Powell to set sail again almost immediately to visit a friend, the Governor of a Dutch settlement at Essequibo on the South American mainland, to obtain seeds and plants of crops suitable for cultivation in the climate and soil of Barbados.[7]

Early reports state that Henry Powell had with him on his first arrival in Barbados eighty settlers, and ten Negro slaves taken from a captured prize,[8] while a later deposition refers to "fifty people well fitted and provided to possess, plant and inhabit the said islands."[9] Whether or not the discrepancy in the figures indicates a differentiation between masters and servants is not clear; what is certain is that some, at least, of this first shipment were servants. Powell himself, in a statement referring to his arrival and subsequent departure for Essequibo, declared:

> Your peticoner in the month of february in the aforesaid year took possession of this island of Barbados and settled here 40 men or more and left my brothers son John Powell Gouvernour; and having left the aforesaid servants upon this Iland I proceeded on my voyage.[10]

In May 1627 two more ships arrived, "freighted with Men and Women Servants."[11] In August of that year, and again in October, Henry Winthrop wrote to relations in England asking them to send him two or three servants.[12] Other references, such as the arrival of Thomas Parris in July 1628 with several servants,[13] suggest that at this stage the flow was already under way. It was no doubt augmented by the several groups of men who arrived, presumably also with servants, under the authority of Sir William Courteen's rival claimant to the proprietorship of the island, the Earl of Carlisle. The latter, after his claim was confirmed in May 1629, was concerned mainly to make money out of the colony. To this end he sent out, under the control of overseers, servants recruited from the lowest levels of the English labouring classes at a price of a few shillings a head.[14]

Once the immediate problems of food and shelter were solved, the settlers soon became aware of the assets of the island. These included fish, flesh and fruit for sustenance, materials for building and for utensils, water for drinking, and, most important for its future development, good soil and a climate conducive to the rapid growth of many types of indigenous plants, which were shortly to be augmented by others brought back from the mainland by Captain Henry Powell from his trip to Essequibo. Powell also brought along some thirty Arawaks to advise on plant cultivation.

Captain John Smith, describing the island in the first two or three years of settlement, notes its many assets:

> The Ile ... (consists for) the most part (of) exceeding good ground, abounding with an infinite number of Swine, some Turtles, and many sortes of excellent fish, many great ponds wherein is Ducke and Mallard; excellent clay for pots, wood and stone for building; and a spring neere the middest of the Ile of Bitume, which is a liquid mixture like Tarre .... The Mancinell apple, is of a most pleasant sweet smell, of the bignesse of a Crab, but ranke poyson ... great store of exceeding great Locus trees ... that beareth a cod full of meal, will make bread in time of necessity. A tree like a Pine, beareth a fruit so great as a Muske Melon ... which will refresh two or three men ... Plumb trees many, the fruit great and yellow ... wilde figge trees there are many ... Gwane trees beare a fruit so bigge as a Peare ... Palmetaes of three severall sorts, Papawes; Prickle peares ... Cedar trees very tall and great; Fusticke trees are very great and the wood yellow, good for dying; sope berries, the kernell so big as a sloe, and good to eat; Pumpeons in abundance; Goads so great as will make good great bottles, and cut in two pieces good dishes and platters; many small brooks of very good water; Ginni wheat, Cassado, Pines and Plantaines ... Tobacco; the corne pease, and beanes, cut but away the stalke, young sprigs will grow, and so bear fruit for many yeares together, without any more planting.[15]

In practical terms, Courteen's men, according to a report written some years later, had by mid 1627 cut the wood to clear the ground some six or seven miles into the island, built at least a hundred houses, and started five plantations. The latter contained, in addition to the indigenous plants, plantains, potatoes and cassava for local consumption, and tobacco and cotton for export.[16] While there is some doubt as to whether the settlers had adequate tools for doing very much clearing of the ground by cutting rather than by burning the wood, while the houses might perhaps be more accurately described as huts or cabins, and while the quality of the tobacco exported left much to be desired, the settlers had, nevertheless, with the assistance of their servants, achieved some considerable measure of success within the space of a few months. This was partly, at least, because of the natural advantages of the island, which, again according to John Smith, was "most healthfull, and all things planted there does increase abundantly."

The weakness caused by the existence of serious rivalries resulting from the Courteen/Carlisle controversy was, however, having its effect, though even John Smith could not be very precise: "there have been so many factions amongst them, I cannot from so many variable relations give you any certainty for their orderly government." This confusion, combined with a serious drought in 1629, and the obvious practical problems inherent in establishing a new settlement, brought about so unhappy a situation that the years 1630 and 1631 were known as the "Starving Time." A visitor to Barbados in 1631, Sir Henry Colt, while extolling its natural advantages and abundance of flora and fauna in much the same terms as Captain John Smith, nevertheless found the plantations, after only three years or so of existence, ruined for lack of care:

> In ten days' travel about them, I never saw any men at work. Your ground and plantation show what you are, they lie like the ruins of some village lately burned; here a great timber tree half burned, in another place a rafter singed all black, there stand a shrub of a tree above two yards high, all the earth covered black with cinders, nothing is clear, what digged or weeded for beauty? All are bushes and long grass, all things carrying the face of a desolate and disorderly show to the beholder.

This, he found, was to a large extent the result of excessive drinking and quarrelling, which could well have been overcome: "You are all young men, and of good desert, if you but bridle the excess of drinking, together with the quarrelsome conditions of your fiery spirits."[17]

In spite of these difficulties, news of which would certainly have filtered back to England and penetrated to some extent to other than official and business circles, the flow of immigration continued apace. However, previous estimates of a population of some 1,500 to 1,600 by about 1628, 1,850 by 1629 and 6,000 by 1636[18] now appear, in the light of recently discovered evidence, to have been exaggerated. A new estimate, based on poll-tax returns for the years 1635 to 1639, suggests that Barbados started more slowly but grew rapidly in the late 1630s to reach a figure somewhere in the region of 10,000 by 1640.[19] Nevertheless, this represents an impressive rate of population growth, indicating that the emigration from England which made this possible had an impetus of its own, as with most other migratory movements. At any rate, the reasons for it should be sought in factors lying mainly on that side of the ocean, some of which would have been rational, but many of which would also have been largely emotional.

Conditions in England at that time were by no means prosperous: an uncertain political situation was to lead to the Civil War in 1642, and the resulting economic conditions, exacerbated by an ever increasing land hunger, were highly depressed. Nevertheless, it obviously required more than adverse political and economic conditions, which had obtained before, as they would again, to provide the motivation necessary to encourage people to seek the unknown. Why should they give up the certainty, albeit a not very prosperous certainty, of their home country, with family and other ties, and make an uncomfortable, quite possibly dangerous, journey across the high seas to a country about which they knew little, and from which they could not be sure of gaining anything?

The answer seems to lie in the massive propaganda campaign which was being waged at that time to encourage people to emigrate and take part in the foundation of an Empire which, it was hoped, would provide opportunities and wealth both for those at home and, perhaps more particularly, for those who ventured abroad in pursuit of this aim. Texts from the Bible were being quoted to encourage people to seek new lands, tracts were being issued and sermons preached to promote the Virginia Company's colony, and Captain John Smith's travel writings were being discussed even by those who could not read. It was an age of adventure, of looking outwards to new experiences, and this, far more than any first hand reports received of conditions in Barbados, must have been what fired the imagination not only of persons of substance, but also to a large extent of persons of lesser condition.

There is ample evidence, from lists still in existence of persons leaving England for the colonies during these years, to confirm that a large proportion of the inhabitants of Barbados were, or had been, indentured servants. Most of these people were poor, and therefore they would inevitably be going to work in that capacity. Indeed, in December 1634, following the establishment in April of the Lords Commissioners for the Plantations, it was ordered that no subsidy men—that is, persons liable to pay subsidy and hence men of means or substance—were to be allowed to emigrate. In addition no one under that degree could leave without a licence from two Justices of the Peace, attesting that he had taken the Oaths of Supremacy and Allegiance, and a certificate from the Minister of his parish, vouching for his religious conformity.[20]

The lists of people leaving England for the plantations in the years immediately following this order make reference specifically to its implementation. In the case of the ship *Ann and Elizabeth*, which left London for Barbados and St. Kitts on 27 April 1635 with eighty-nine men and nineteen women on board, it is carefully pointed out that among them were "no Subsedy Men, whereof they brought test: from the Minister of St. Kathrin's neere ye Tower of London." In April 1639 the *Virgin* left Southampton for Barbados with a varied group of "tradesmen," boys and servant-maids, about whom it was stated that "these and the former which pass in this ship were not Subsidy men, but people and servants of meane condition." The total number of persons listed as leaving from London in the year 1635 was 707 men and 36 women for Barbados, and 191 men and 21 women for Barbados and St. Kitts, which no doubt represented only a small proportion of the overall numbers leaving England in these years. In only one case in these lists, however, is there a reference to persons of substance, and this was to three "gentlemen free planters of Barbados" who, with their five servants, were to go to Guernsey on 28 June 1639 to transship for Barbados.[21]

In addition to the emigrants from England, a number of Irish found their way to Barbados. Their numbers are likely to have been far greater than is suggested by the contemporary evidence, if the trouble they caused the authorities in the next few decades is any criterion. Father Andrew White, a Jesuit priest who visited Barbados in 1634 on his way to Maryland wrote: "some few Catholiques here be, both English and Irish,"[22] and in 1637 a London merchant rounded up, in and around Kinsdale in Ireland, some fifty-six servants, including twenty women, and shipped them off to Barbados.[23]

Most of these emigrants, with the probable exception of the Irish, appear to have left their homes without any overt coercion. Developments over the next few years were, however, foreshadowed in a request made in April 1642 by Thomas Verney, a ne'er-do-well son of a distinguished family who had been despatched to seek his fortune in the West Indies, that his father should procure him a hundred men with the help of "brideswell and the prisons."[24]

The majority of these people leaving their homes for the uncertainty of a new life in an unknown environment, although certainly poor, were drawn mainly from the class of skilled labourers and artisans. The group which left Southampton for Barbados in April 1639, for example, was comprised of eight husbandmen, two sergeweavers, two persons described as servants, two tailors, two shoemakers and a hoopmaker, cordwayner, smith, ropemaker, barber, chandler, seaman, currier, glover and clothworker.[25] There would, of course, be no guarantee that they would be able to practice their particular skills once they got to their destination, but many of these were much in demand on the plantations. Thomas Verney, writing to his father on 21 September 1640, asked for "twenty able men-servants whereof two to be carpenters, two of them to be joyners and two sayers, all of them to have their tools belonging to their several occupations."[26]

Once these emigrants had reached Barbados it seems unlikely that their families and friends in England received much in the way of information from them. Communications were difficult and there was no regular letter post, even if the persons directly involved were able to read and write. The voyage to Barbados, therefore, for the average indentured servant, must have been a journey of no return in more ways than one. If, indeed, they had been able to communicate with those left behind in England, and if they had reported accurately, the indentured servant would have described a life of extreme hardship. This was the case not only as far as the work of clearing the land and planting and hoeing and weeding it in the broiling sun was concerned, but also the unsatisfactory conditions of life owing to the inadequate implementation of the terms of indenture and the cruelty of many of the masters.

It appears that there was some form of indenture in operation from the beginning of the settlement. This is confirmed in letters from Henry Winthrop to his relations in England. He announced in a letter to his uncle, dated 22 August 1627: "I do intend, God willing, to stay here on this iland called the Barbathes, in the West Indies, and here I and my servantes to joine in plantinge of tobaccoe ... and I doe intend to have everye yere some 2 or 3 servantes over, and to have them bound to me for 3 yeres for so muche a yere, some 5 lbs or 6 lbs a yere, and there allwayes to have a plantation of servantes." He asked his father, John Winthrop, on 15 October 1627, to "send me over sum 2 or 3 men ye they be bound to searve me in the West Indies some 3 yere or 5, wch you doe thincke good to binde them for, and get them as reasonable as you can, promysinge them not above 10 pd a yere, and a chest of conveniensie for clothese."[27]

In addition to references to the period of service and the amount of regular payment, the indentures normally included provision for food, clothing and accommodation. An agreement dated 25 October 1637 concerns William Hall, a planter who had evidently fallen on hard times, and who was to be indentured to Arthur Yeomans, "Gent.," "to serve him for four years ... Yeomans to find and allow Hall, meat, drink, apparell and lodging with other necessaryes during the said tearme."[28] An indication of the type of housing was given by Thomas Verney when he wrote that he was "building a sorry cottage to harbour the men";[29] while the sort of clothing to be given them was described in his order for "twelve dozen of drawers; as many shirts and shoes. Four dozen munmoth capps. Four dozen of cours neck cloths. Two dozen of broad hose, as many narrow hose."[30]

The planter, therefore, was obligated to provide generally for the servant during his period of indenture. What, however, is not clear is the very important question of whether or not the indentured servant on his release received a plot of land. There are references to a law allowing three, four, or five acres to a servant who had served his time, though there is no trace of the law itself.[31] A declaration made by the Earl of Carlisle in 1647, providing for freemen, who had no land in Barbados, to be alloted land in Nevis, Antigua or other islands within his proprietorship, implies that there had been some understanding that land would be available to servants in Barbados, though the wording concerning the terms is somewhat ambiguous:

> Whereas divers people have been transplanted from the Kingdom of England to my Island of Barbados in America, and have there remained a long time as Servants in great labour for the profits of other persons, upon whose Account they were first conveyed thither, expecting after their fruitful service, according to the Covenants agreed upon at their first entrance, there to make some advantage to themselves by the settling

Plantations for their own use, but by reason of the great
number of people who repaired thither ... the land is taken up
as there is not any more to be had but at great rates too high for
the purchase of poor servants.[32]

There is, in fact, little evidence that any grants of land of this kind were ever
made and the practice may well have fallen into abeyance at a very early
date. An agreement, for example, of 25 October 1637 refers only to the
provision of 400 pounds of "good and merchantable cotton, or tobacco" at
the end of four years' indenture.[33]

Just as the position concerning the provision of land seems to have been, at
best, equivocal, the agreements to provide board and lodging, although
clearly expressed, were by no means always satisfactorily implemented.
Thomas Verney again throws light on conditions in a letter of 1639, stating
that potatoes were "the best provision we have in the land, both for ourselves
and servants, but chiefly for them, for they will not desire, after a month or
two, noe other provision but potatoes boyled, and mobby to drink with
them—and this we call mobby is only potatoes boyled, and then pressed." On
Verney's own showing this was rather an odd statement, as in the same letter
he describes the fruit growing on the island: "oranges, lemons, limes,
plantines, guaves ... pepper, cinnamon, ginger ... the last and best fruit is
your pineapple," while also mentioning the existence of land crabs.[34] One is
left to wonder why the servants could not have made use of what was
obviously available, as well as what had become of all the fish, flesh and fruit
described by Captain John Smith as having been so abundant some ten years
previously.

The treatment of servants by their masters was generally poor. Sir William
Tufton, who arrived as Governor in September 1629, became extremely
unpopular with the planters on account of his attacks on them for their
barbarous treatment of their servants.[35] He appears to have had little success,
if the following case, reported in the Minutes of Council in May 1640, is in
any way typical:

Francis Leaven and his brother-in-law, Ensign Samuel Hodgkynns did inhumanely and unchristian-like torture John
Thomas, a Servant, by hanging him up by the hands, and
putting fired matches between his fingers, whereby he hath lost
the use of his right hand. Ordered: Leaven and Hodgkynns to
pay John Thomas, within ten days, 5,000 lbs of cotton apiece,
and Thomas to be immediately free from his master. Leaven to
take a speedy course for the curing of Thomas and for payment
of the same Leaven and Hodgkynns to remain in prison during
the law's pleasure.[36]

Given these conditions, it was small wonder that little cooperation with their masters was forthcoming from the servants and that Sir Henry Colt was able to complain in 1631 that "your servants also you keep too idly. They continually passed our Ship without any occasion or acquaintance, lingering sometimes 24 hours with us ... to avoid labour."[37] Indeed, three years later, this dissatisfaction showed itself in a conspiracy, the first of two serious manifestations of deep-seated disaffection among white servants. Father Andrew White recounted, in connection with his visit to Barbados in 1634, how his ship managed to avoid possible interception at Bonavista by a Spanish fleet, and went on to say:

> In the meantime we were rescued from a greater danger at Barbados, for the servants through the whole island conspired for the slaughter of their masters, and when they should assert their liberty successfully, resolved to seize the first ship which should arrive and put out to sea. The conspiracy having been discovered by one whom the atrocity of the deed deterred, the execution of one of the leaders served for the security of the island and for our safety; for our ship, as it was the first that reached the shore, had been destined for their prey and on the very day on which we landed we found eight hundred men under arms in order to prevent this most imminent crime.[38]

No doubt it was another manifestation of this same discontent that caused the indentured labourer at quite an early stage to look for new fields outside Barbados. In the years 1638 to 1642, several hundred men left for Tobago, St. Lucia and Hispaniola.[39] The figure was small, compared with the number of immigrants, but this was one of several features of those early years which were to be repeated, on a much larger scale, in the future.

Chapter 2
Consolidated Immigration (1643–1659)

During the 1640s Barbados underwent its first revolution, as significant in its own way as the industrial revolution in England, for the effect it was to have on the whole of its future political, economic and social development. This was its switch from the cultivation of mixed crops on comparatively small farms with few labourers to that of sugar cane on large plantations with an extensive labour force. The immediate need in those early years of the plantation system, when the importation of slaves from Africa was only a trickle, was for labour, and the obvious source of that labour was still the mother country. Fortunately for the planters, conditions in England during the 1640s and 1650s were such as to encourage emigration, both voluntary and forced, and thus augment considerably the stream of indentured servants which was already leaving the country.

The "regular" indentured servants no doubt provided the most satisfactory section of the labour force. With the growth of the settlement, the need for persons trained in various trades increased. Richard Ligon, who provided a precise and detailed description of the main features of the island and its life during his stay from 1647 to 1650, advised potential planters to take servants with them, particularly "trades-men, as Carpenters, Joiners, Masons, Smiths, Paviers and Coopers."[1] In fact, the lists of persons leaving Bristol for Foreign Plantations during the years 1654 to 1686 show that many of the emigrants possessed special skills. For example, among the total of over a thousand males leaving for Barbados between 1655 and 1660, some sixty different occupations were specified. Of these, the most heavily represented were those concerned with agriculture, including yeomen, husbandmen and labourers, but there were also many connected with the clothing industry, such as buttonmakers, clothiers, clothworkers, dyers, glovers, shoemakers, silk-weavers, tailors, weavers and woosted-combers. Many were connected with the building trade, including bricklayers, carpenters, glaziers, joiners, plasterers, sawyers, tilers; and with other less obviously useful trades, in the context of Barbados, such as coalminers and pewterers. Of interest also are the details provided, albeit somewhat sporadically, of the places of origin of these emigrants. Naturally enough, for reasons not only of geography but of politics, the area best represented is the west of England; but it is worth noting, especially for the benefit of those who see a west-country man lurking inside every Barbadian, that almost all the counties of England and Wales, with the exception mainly of the four northernmost counties, and seven of the counties of Ireland, appear on these lists.[2]

At the same time as this voluntary emigration was in progress, a very different type of exodus was taking place. Cromwell, whose victories in England, Scotland and Ireland had encumbered him with prisoners of war, was in the process of shipping his captives off to Barbados and elsewhere, and this on a large scale and with considerable brutality. The arrangements for this transfer were formalized in 1648, when a committee of the House of Commons recommended that a system of warrants for the transportation of prisoners be introduced.[3] By 1655 a total of twelve thousand prisoners of war was alleged by the planters of Barbados to be employed by them, which would have represented nearly half the total white population of the island at the time.[4] These prisoners included those taken at the battles of Preston and Colchester in 1648, during the Irish Rebellion of 1649 and after the battles of Dunbar and Worcester in 1650 and 1651.

Barbados was obviously regarded by Cromwell as a convenient dumping ground for prisoners whom he would otherwise have found an embarrassment. Some indication of this is given in a letter from him dated 17 September 1649 to the Speaker of the Parliament of England, referring to the storming of Drogheda in Ireland: "When they submitted, their officers were knocked on the head; and every tenth man of the soldiers killed; and the rest shipped for the Barbadoes. The soldiers in the other Tower were all spared, as to their lives only, and shipped likewise for the Barbadoes."[5] This wholesale transshipment of bodies in fact gave rise to a new verb in the English language, "to barbadoes." A letter of 11 March 1655, concerning the Salisbury uprising at the end of 1654, noted that "several were hanged; a great many 'sent to Barbadoes.' ... A terrible Protector this ... He dislikes shedding blood, but is very apt 'to barbadoes' an unruly man—has sent and sends us by hundreds to Barbadoes, so that we have made an active verb of it: 'Barbadoes you.'"[6]

Indeed, in this uprising at Salisbury, seventy Royalist gentlemen, including "officers, gentlemen and divines" and one respectable Devonshire country gentleman aged seventy-six, were arrested on suspicion of complicity in the uprising, brought to trial but not convicted, and, after a year in prisons in Exeter and Ilchester, were suddenly removed to Plymouth, placed on a ship, and after ten days at anchor and five weeks and four days at sea, found themselves in Barbados. The conditions on board were appalling: "the captive prisoners being all the way locked up under decks ... among horses,

that their souls, through heat and steam, under the tropic, fainted in them."
On arrival they were sold for 1550 pounds of sugar per man. Their treatment
as indentured servants was intolerable:

> They now generally grinding at the mills and attending at the
> furnaces, or digging in the scorching island; having nothing to
> feed on (notwithstanding their hard labour) but potatoe roots,
> nor to drink, but water with such roots washed in it ... being
> bought and sold still from one master to another, or attached as
> horses and beasts for the debts of their masters, being whipped
> at the whipping post (as rogues) for their masters pleasure, and
> sleeping in sties worse than hogs in England.

This description formed part of a petition entitled *England's Slavery, or
Barbados Merchandise* drawn up by two of the group, Marcellus Rivers and
Oxenbridge Foyle, which was heard in the House of Commons on 25 March
1659. In replying, the High Sheriff of Devon justified his actions as having
been carried out on the instructions of "his late Highness." Martin Noell,
whose name crops up frequently in the context of arranging shipments of men
to the colonies, also countered that the description of conditions was
exaggerated. They work, he said, "but from six to six: so it is not so hard as
is represented to you: not so much as the common herdsman here. The work
is mostly carried on by the negroes."[7]

One section of the group evidently took the law into their own hands and,
not being prepared to put up with the fate they realised awaited them,
arranged to buy their freedom even before they set foot in the island. Once
there, they travelled around the island spreading sedition; they went "from
plantacon to plantacon to discourage servants from that service and
obedience they owe ... to their Masters. Mistresses and Overseers and
endeavour to beget in them mutinous and seditious thoughts and to draw
them if they might into rebellious practices by insinuating and spreading
amongst them ... false reports and misinformation of things acted and done
by the supreame authorities of ye Commonwealth of England."[8] No doubt at
the Restoration many of those who had managed to survive their ordeal were
able to make their way back to England.

Cromwell was also responsible for initiating the transportation to the
colonies of convicts and other "undesirables." In England this appears to
have started about 1654, with the despatching to Barbados of pirates caught
on the high seas, and to have been extended some two years later when the
Council of State promulgated orders concerning the apprehending of "lewd
and dangerous persons, rogues, vagrants, and other idle persons, who have no
way of livelihood, and refuse to work," and arrangements for transporting
them to the "English Plantations in America."[9] This practice was, however,
evidently carried out on a far larger scale in Ireland; in 1654 the governors
of several Irish counties had orders "to arrest all wanderers, men and women,

and such other Irish within their precincts as should not prove they had a
settled course of industry as yielded a means of their own to maintain them,
all such children as were in hospitals or workhouses, all prisoners, men and
women, to be transported to the West Indies."[10] The next year the transportation of Catholic priests from Ireland was under way; those in custody in
Dublin, but not found guilty of murder, were to be transported to Barbados
and those under the age of forty were to be shipped to Barbados and other
American plantations.[11] Thus the number of Irish reaching Barbados must
have been considerable, and within a year or two they were causing the
authorities great concern.

Yet another method of supplying the ever-increasing demands of the
colonies for labour, whilst simultaneously lining the pockets of those involved
in the business of transshipment, was that of "spiriting." This involved
enticing away persons, frequently youths and even children, by a combination
of the use of force, bribes and false promises. Already in 1645 an Ordinance of
Parliament had instructed the appropriate authorities to apprehend all
persons concerned with the traffic in children.[12] In 1656 soldiers of the
London garrison were reported to have visited brothels and other places of ill
repute and press-ganged four hundred women of loose life to join several
hundreds already on board a ship leaving for Barbados.[13] In 1657 an official
search of a ship leaving for the West Indies discovered eleven persons "taken
by the pirates" and all those who wished were allowed to disembark.[14]

The many thousands of indentured servants reaching Barbados during these
years were thus extremely varied as to their political, economic, social and
religious backgrounds. Generally speaking, it is fair to say that the waves of
immigration of other than regular indentured servants had brought to
Barbados a mass of people, most of whom, for a variety of reasons, were
unlikely to submit readily to the hard work of the plantation, and some of
whom were patently from the criminal and near criminal classes. Even in
Ligon's time some of the women on his ship, who were also destined for
Barbados, were allegedly "taken from Bridewel, Turnball Street, and suchlike
places of education."[15] By 1654 Henry Whistler was writing his classic words:
"This Illand is the Dunghill wharone England doth cast forth its rubidg:
Rodgs and hors and such like people, are those which are gennerally Brought
heare: a Baud brought ouer puts one a demour comportment a whore if
hansume makes a wife for sume rich planter."[16] Whatever their original
backgrounds, however, the circumstances of the employment of the indentured servants and the conditions under which they lived must soon have
reduced many, though by no means all of them, to a uniform state of abject
misery.

The actual conditions of service did not differ very much from those of the
previous period. An attempt was made, however, to codify some of the
practices relating to servants and a law was passed in Barbados in 1652
providing for servants who had made no contracts in England to serve for

seven years if they were under eighteen, and five years if they were over eighteen, and to receive four hundred pounds of sugar at the end of their service.[17] Examples of contracts drawn up in England after that time showed that there was little attempt at coordination among the bondmasters there and between them and those in Barbados. Edward Jones, a farrier from Monmouthshire, was bound at Bristol in 1656 "for three years to serve in Barbados and to have at the end thereof thirteen pounds sterling, two suites of apparrell and one thereof of Canvas and the other of Woolen, Fower shirts of Dowlass, Fower paires of Woolen knit stockings, one hatt, and two neckcloths." On the other hand, John Apperley, a yeoman from Hereford, was indentured on 12 January 1659 to serve for five years and at the end to receive five pounds sterling.[18]

No doubt conflicts frequently arose over interpretations in Barbados of contracts drawn up in England as well as over the implementation of the contracts. In any case, the extent to which the servant received what was due to him would depend very much on the attitude of the master. As one writer put it at the beginning of the 1650s: "It is the Custome for a Christian Servant to serve foure yeares, and then enjoy his freedome: and (which hee hath dearly earned) 10 l. Ster. or the value of it in goods if his Master bee soe honest as to pay it."[19]

The importance of the attitude of the masters for the well-being, or otherwise, of the servants is amply confirmed by Ligon:

> As for the usage of the Servants, it is much as the Master is, merciful or cruel; Those that are merciful, treat their Servants well, both in their meat, drink, and lodging, and give them such work as is not unfit for Christians to do. But if the Masters be cruel, the Servants have very wearisome and miserable lives.

He goes on to describe their everyday lives, from the time of their arrival:

> Upon the arrival of any ship ... the Planters go aboard; and having bought such of them as they like, send them with a guid to his Plantation; and being come, commands them instantly to make their Cabins, which they not knowing how to do, are to be advised by other of their servants, that are their Seniors; but, if they be churlish, and will not show them, or if materials be wanting to make them Cabins, then they are to lye on the ground that night. These Cabins are to be made of sticks, withs, and Plantine leaves, under some little shade that may keep the rain off; their Suppers being a few Potatoes for meat, and water or Mobbie for drink. The next day they are rung out with a Bell to work, at six a clock in the morning ... till the Bell ring again, which is at eleven a clock; and then they return and are set to dinner, either with a mess of Lob-lolly, Bonavist, or Potatoes.

At one a clock, they are rung out again to the field, there to
work till six, and then home again, to a supper of the same. And
if it chance to rain, and wet them through, they have no shift,
but must lye so all night.

If they made any complaint, Ligon revealed, even in case of sickness, they
were likely to be beaten by the Overseer and, if they resisted, their period of
indenture very likely doubled:

I have seen an Overseer beat a Servant with a cane about the
head, till the blood has followed, for a fault that is not worth
the speaking of; and yet he must have patience, or worse will
follow. Truly, I have seen such cruelty there done to Servants,
as I did not think one Christian could have done to another.

Conditions, however, were said to have been improving somewhat:

For now most of the servants lie in Hamocks, and in warm
rooms, and when they come in wet, have shift of shirts and
drawers ... and are fed with bone meat twice or thrice a week.
Collonel Walrond seeing his servants when they came home,
toyled with their labour, and wet through with their sweating
... resolved therefore to send into England for rug Gowns ...
that so when they shifted themselves, they might put on those
gowns, and lie and rest in their Hamocks.

Indeed, if Ligon had had his way, conditions would have been still further
improved. His very detailed specifications for equipping a plantation included
provision for the servants to receive, in addition to the usual clothes, Irish
rugs and stockings and twelve pairs of shoes a year, and for beef, pork and
salt fish to supplement their diet.[21]

However, the general impression of continuing improvement suggested by
Ligon must be tempered in the light not only of the experiences of the
Salisbury group of Royalists, but also of the evidence provided by contemporary legislation. Inevitably, in view of the position already noted in which
the servant, at least for the period of his indenture, was virtually the chattel of
his master, the first items of legislation concerning the relations between
masters and indentured servants make ample provision for safeguarding the
rights of the masters but pay scant attention to the grievances of the servants.
The collection of Acts and Statutes enacted after the surrender of Barbados to
the Commonwealth, in 1652, contained six items concerned with restricting
the movements, business activities, sex lives and marriages of the servants,
and protecting their masters against violence and theft. There were,
however, but three items relating to the welfare of servants. These concerned
the masters' responsibilities for servants in case of sickness and for the
payment of wages and, most important, provision for examination by Justices

of the Peace in the event of disputes over the lengths of service of the latter. At the same time, there was nothing whatever to protect the servants against acts of violence or any other form of ill treatment from their masters.[21]

In this situation it is not surprising that, in spite of the exhausting nature of the work carried out by the servants, the inadequacy of their diet and the restrictions upon their movements, they took various opportunities of revenging, or attempting to revenge, themselves upon their masters. Burning of cane was much indulged in by servants "to the utter ruin and undoing of their Masters." In 1649 this dissatisfaction and desire for revenge reached such a point that some of them made plans to band together, kill their masters and take over the island. Ligon writes of this conspiracy:

> Their sufferings being grown to a great height, and their daily complainings to one another ... being spread throughout the Island; at the last, some amongst them, whose spirits were not able to endure such slavery, resolved to break through it, or dye in the act; and so conspired with some others ... so that a day was appointed to fall upon their Masters, and cut all their throats, and by that means, to make themselves not only freemen, but Masters of the Island. And so closely was this plot carried, as no discovery was made, till the day before they were to put it in act: and then one of them, either by the failing of his courage, or some new obligation from the love of his Master, revealed the long plotted conspiracy; and so by this timely advertisement, the Masters were saved.[22]

As has already been indicated, the Irish in particular were a serious nuisance to the authorities. As early as 1644, well before the influx of Irish transported on the instructions of Cromwell began, an act was passed "for the prohibition of landing Irish persons."[23] When Admiral Penn and General Venables came to Barbados in 1655 to collect troops for their projected expedition to Hispaniola, they found that many of the recruits were Irish, but that they were "a profligate race, who were in the habit of joining themselves to Runaway Slaves."[24]

Two years later, action to disarm them and restrict their activities was taken on two counts. In September 1657 an Order in Council was issued, referring to the "considerable number of Irish freemen and servants within this Island" and the dangers inherent in allowing them, and "such others as are of the Romish religion," to have arms and ammunition at a time when the Commonwealth of England was at war with Spain, and ordering them to be disarmed forthwith. In addition, they were regarded as dangerous in a purely local context. A proclamation, of the same date, noted that many of the Irish "doe wander up and down from plantation to plantation as vagabonds refusing to labour or put themselves in any service but continuinge in

a dissolute and sloathful kind of life putt themselves on evil practises as pil-
ferings, thefts, roberyes and other felonious acts." In view of the fact that
they were encouraging others in their bad ways, and possibly also fomenting
rebellion, it was ordered that, in addition to disarming them, special precau-
tions should be taken against their visiting plantations without good reason.[25]
Moreover, in 1660, shortly before the Acts relating to the disarming of the
Irish were ordered to be repealed, church wardens were instructed to take an
exact list of all the Irish in their several parishes and return the names of
"turbulent and dangerous spirits."[26]

It will have been noted that these references to the Irish mention both freemen and servants. Indeed, during this time of approximately forty years, indentures were expiring and former servants, whatever their places of origin,
were finding themselves on the labour market. Some, for lack of other opportunities, reindentured themselves, others worked as hired servants, while
some continued to practice their special skills, though to an ever decreasing
extent. Slaves were already at that time beginning to do some of the sugar
boiling and other artisans' work formerly done by the indentured labourers.[27]
This set a pattern in the relationship between planters, poor whites and

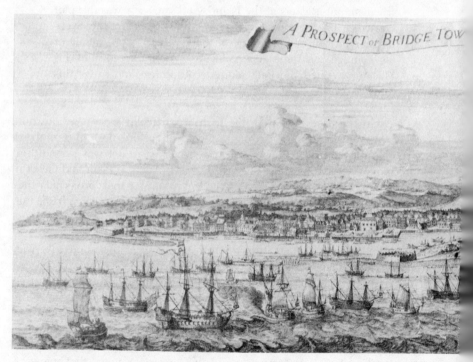

A Prospect of Bridgetown in Barbados

slaves—and later the free coloureds—which was to continue, with variations, well into the nineteenth century. Thus, whereas the planter was concerned only with his own profit, the poor white lacked the inclination and the energy to do anything about improving, or even maintaining, his position; and while slaves had to do what they were told, the energy and undaunted ability possessed by many of them were gradually coming to the fore. The emergence of this pattern marked the beginning of a long process of deterioration in the situation of the poor white which was to become increasingly evident during the course of the next two hundred years.

The lack of employment opportunities, added to the near impossibility of the poor man's obtaining land, caused the inclination towards emigration, already becoming evident in the previous period, to increase considerably. The total emigration figure at this stage has been assessed, though possibly too generously, at some ten thousand. About half went to the mainland American colonies, various of the Windward and Leeward Islands and to Surinam, while the other half went to Jamaica.[28] Indeed, Cromwell, who was fired with enthusiasm for his "Western Design," which saw the settlement of Jamaica as an important strategic point in the grandiose plan of taking over

(By courtesy of the Barbados Museum and Historical Society)

the territories held by Spain in the Caribbean, became personally involved in trying to get people from Barbados and the Leeward Islands to go to Jamaica. He had some limited success in Barbados, where the shortage of land generated considerable enthusiasm among former indentured servants.[29] This was only achieved, however, with some difficulty, in view of the reported high death rate in Jamaica and, up to a point, against the better judgement of the Governor of Barbados, who considered that the numbers which had departed by late 1656 "hath much weakened the strength of this place, for that most of them were freemen, which is the safety of the island, next under the divine providence, that protecteth us amongst so many slaves and servants we here have."[30]

Nevertheless, in spite of this emigration, and a high mortality rate, the flood of white immigrants succeeded in maintaining a significant rate of increase in the white population. Even if one estimate of the white population's having remained constant during this period at a figure of about thirty thousand is exaggerated,[31]—a figure of twenty thousand by 1660 seems more accurate[32]—this still represented a very considerable influx of white servants. This trend was to be reversed in the next few years, however, causing later governors of Barbados to echo Governor Searle's words of 1656, and to make repeated, if mainly unsuccessful, attempts to encourage the importation of the white servants they thought were essential to the island, both internally as a defence against possible insurrection by the slaves, and externally as a bulwark against potential attacks by foreign foes.

Chapter 3
Decline in the White Population (1660–1703)

Barbados in the 1660s and 1670s has been described as the richest colony in English America.[1] Certainly its planters were rich and were living in a style undreamt of before the days of sugar. One account, written in 1666, described the buildings as "very fair and beautiful, and their houses like castles."[2] By 1695, if a print of that date provides an accurate representation of the scene, Bridgetown was a city of substantial and even elegant buildings, the countryside behind the town heavily cultivated, and Carlisle Bay filled with ships going about their business of bringing in food and other supplies and transporting away the products of the island.[3]

Nevertheless, the Restoration in 1660 marks the first beginnings of a gradual decline in the fortunes of Barbados. On the political scene, the extraordinary degree of independence, amounting virtually to dominion status, which was achieved during the latter years of the Commonwealth was lost at the Restoration. The reimposition of a form of proprietary government, with the King as Proprietor, may have removed some of the abuses of the old system but it brought with it many of the disadvantages of control from abroad by persons with little knowledge of the local scene. In the economic sphere, the reenactment of the Navigation Acts, which restricted the carrying of all products to and from the colonies to English ships, had a serious effect on trade. In addition, the levying of a $4\frac{1}{2}$ percent tax on all exported commodities caused considerable hardship, particularly at times when the sugar crop fell below standard. There were also, during the second half of the seventeenth century, various natural disasters, ranging from plagues of locusts and caterpillars which damaged crops, and serious fires which burnt down much of Bridgetown, to hurricanes which wrought serious havoc throughout the island. The general impression conveyed during the last four decades of the century was of a gradually declining situation, indicated in the overall decrease in the numbers of white servants and landless freemen shown by such scanty figures as are available and, perhaps rather more dramatically, by the concern evidenced, and the action taken, both in England and later in

27

Barbados, to attempt to rectify the situation.

In England an attempt was made to regularise the transportation of emigrants and to prevent abuses through the setting up of the Council for Foreign Plantations in 1660. The Council was instructed to consider how the colonies might best be supplied with servants, how those who were willing to go might be encouraged, how those who were unwilling might be prevented from being transported illegally, and how proper legal arrangements might be made for sending away vagrants and others "who remain here noxious and unprofitable."[4] During 1664 various proposals resulted from this. An office was to be set up for registering all persons going voluntarily to the plantations. By this means it was hoped to prevent "spiriting" as well as malpractices on the part of the merchants.[5] A further attempt to prevent spiriting was made in 1671, when an Act was passed to prevent the stealing and transporting of children,[6] and again in 1682, when the Privy Council, in order to tighten up the requirements for registration, decreed that prospective servants must be bound in the presence of a Justice of the Peace or Chief Magistrate.[7] Another proposal resulting directly from the instructions to the Council was for the constituting of an office "to transport to the Plantations all vagrants, rogues and idle persons that can give no account of themselves, felons who have the benefit of clergy, such as are convicted of petty larceny, vagabonds, gypsies and loose persons, making resort to unlicensed brothels."[8] As far as Barbados was concerned, however, these new arrangements did not have much effect as the tide of immigration had already by the early 1660s dwindled into little more than a trickle.

The regular indentured servants, who had previously formed the backbone of the labour force on the plantations in Barbados, had already begun to look elsewhere. The American colonies, as well as Jamaica and Nevis, seemed far more attractive because of the availability of land. Barbados had not only for some time had little spare land, but was also acquiring a bad reputation for the treatment of indentured servants, partly, no doubt, as a result of the publication in 1657 of Ligon's *True and Exact History of the Island of Barbados*. Certainly the number of persons leaving Bristol for Barbados declined considerably; indeed, the total for the fifteen years from 1661 to 1675, after which the flow virtually ceased, was about half what it had been in the six years from 1655 to 1660.[9] Again, the number leaving London for Barbados between the years 1682 and 1692 totalled only ninety-three men and twenty-six women.[10]

The transportation of criminals, notwithstanding the extent to which it had been discussed, seems not to have resulted in any very large numbers of them reaching Barbados, probably in part because of the practical difficulties involved. Christopher Jeaffreson has provided a very detailed account of the financial and logistic problems he encountered during the years 1676 to 1686 when trying to arrange for the transportation of criminals to his plantation in St. Kitts.[11] Presumably the same kinds of difficulties were also met by those interested in sending criminals to Barbados. Similarly, though there were some cases of persons spirited away to Barbados, including one in which four persons complained on arrival in Barbados of having been forcibly transported thither on board the *Mermaid*, and who were subsequently released,[12] there is no evidence that the numbers were very great.

At the same time, there was also a decline in the number of prisoners of war and other political "undesirables" who were available. The political situation in England had changed drastically since the days of the Civil War and Cromwell's victories in the field, when prisoners had provided such a vast reservoir of manpower for the colonies. Nonetheless, troubled conditions in Scotland were responsible for the shipment of unspecified numbers of Scottish rebels to Barbados in 1667, and of thirty or so more after the defeat of the Duke of Argyll in 1685.[13] In the same year, the defeat of the Duke of Monmouth of Sedgemoor resulted in the despatch to Barbados of some four hundred of those of his supporters who had been taken prisoner.

The information available concerning this group is quite considerable, and it is this fact which may have given rise to the popular myth that the present day "Redlegs" are descended from it. The names are available of the 305 persons who reached Barbados alive.[14] There is also information on the particular circumstances of their shipment to Barbados, and the conditions under which they were forced to live when they arrived on the island. Seldom have such careful arrangements been made for the reception of a party of prisoners. Acting on instructions from the King, a bill was drawn up and passed on 4 January 1686, with very strict provisions for insuring that the "Rebels Convict" would serve for ten years; that any attempts to leave the island would be prevented; their transfers to other owners reported; and the possibility of their achieving freedom through marriage frustrated by heavy sentences (for any women involved) of two thousand pounds sterling and six months' imprisonment.[15] Hall, in his edition of the *Acts Passed in the Island of Barbados*, followed the title of the Act in question with a note: "The condition of these Rebels was by this Act made as bad, if not worse, than the Negroes."[16]

The first shipment of the rebels arrived just after the law had been passed. The state of the prisoners when they embarked cannot have been very good; some of them had been wounded in battle, all of them had suffered at the hands of Judge Jeffreys and had spent several months in jail. It is surprising that as many survived the journey as did, considering the conditions aboard the ships in which they were transported. Macaulay, quoting from an account provided by one John Cod, a rebel who was sent to Jamaica, wrote:

> It appears from the best information ... that more than
> one-fifth of those who were shipped were flung to the sharks
> before the end of the voyage. The human cargoes were stowed
> close in the holds of small vessels. So little space was allowed

that the wretches, many of whom were still tormented by
unhealed wounds, could not all lie down at once without lying
on one another. They were never suffered to go on deck. The
hatchway was constantly watched by sentinels armed with
hangers and blunderbusses. In the dungeon below all was
darkness, stench, lamentation, disease and death. The survivors
when they arrived at their house of bondage were mere
skeletons. During some weeks coarse biscuit and fetid water
had been doled out to them in such scanty measure that any
one of them could easily have consumed the ration that was
assigned to five. They were, therefore, in such a state that the
merchant to whom they had been consigned found it expedient
to fatten them before selling them.[17]

One of the rebels sent to Barbados, Henry Pitman, succeeded in escaping
after fifteen months, and gave an account of his experiences. Pitman was a
surgeon who at his trial had pleaded guilty and been sentenced to be "drawn,
hanged and quartered"; this sentence was commuted to transportation. He
thought he had managed to purchase his freedom, and had in fact paid for it,
but on arrival in Barbados he had been sold to a planter. His master used his
services as a surgeon but gave him no payment, whereupon Pitman refused to
function as a surgeon while being treated as a servant. This provoked his
master to hit him about the head with a cane until the latter disintegrated and
to put him in the stocks in the sun, until after twelve hours his mistress,
"moved either with Pitty or Shame gave order for (his) release." His diet,
which included "five Pound of Salt Irish Beef, or Salt Fish a week ... and
Indian or Guiny Corn ground on a stone, and made into Dumplins," he
regarded as "very mean";[18] it was, however, a considerable improvement over
the potatoes and "mobby" diet of previous generations of indentured
servants.

In the event, the Monmouth rebels did not serve their full term. On the
accession of William and Mary to the throne in 1689, the previous Act was
disallowed. This was extremely unpalatable to the planters, who had expected
to have the services of the rebels for ten years and claimed to have trained
them for various specialist tasks. As a result of representations made by the
Governor to the Lords of Trade and Plantations, a compromise was reached[19]
and the act was eventually repealed on 17 March 1691, more than a year after
the original order, in such terms that "Rebels Convict" were freed from their
servitude but forbidden to leave the island without the King's permission,
given no form of reward on completing their service, and forced to serve in
the Militia.[20]

One other category of immigrants reaching Barbados in the 1660s,
probably in larger numbers than before, were the victims of religious
persecution. Some of these were transported for refusing to comply with the

Clarendon Code; many of them would have been Quakers, who bore the brunt of the persecution. Most of the Quakers appear rapidly to have reached positions of some prominence in Barbados, and cannot, therefore, be considered under the heading of indentured servants. Interestingly enough, one shipment of Quakers from Hertford escaped banishment, for a time at least, owing to the superstition and perhaps delicate conscience of the master of the ship in which they were being transported to Barbados and Jamaica. The ship had met with various disasters after the Quakers came on board and the master returned them, judging it contrary to the laws of England to transport men without their consent.[21]

Inevitably, as they completed their terms of service, many of those indentured for political or religious reasons managed either to return home with a change in the regime or to establish themselves in satisfactory circumstances on the island. Nonetheless, the majority of those who had come as regular indentured servants, or as transported criminals, probably lacked the means and the connections to improve their material situation very much as long as they remained in Barbados. Some re-indentured themselves or operated as hired servants, while those who had particular skills tried to practice them in Bridgetown and elsewhere, with a number acquiring small plots of land and cultivating them either on their own or, if they prospered sufficiently, with the help of one or two slaves.

Governor Atkins' census of 1680, in spite of its wealth of detail concerning the lives of the inhabitants of Barbados, contains little information about their occupations. A specific figure is given of 2,317 servants; this includes both indentured and hired white servants. A proportion, perhaps a quarter, of the 405 Bridgetown householders might be poor whites, working at various trades. Most of the 1,186 "freemen," owning less than 10 acres of land along with a few slaves, and sometimes employing a white servant, can be assumed to fall into the category of poor whites. Thus a very approximate estimate of the total number of the poor white males, excluding their families, would be 3,400. The rest of the white island population, including the 1,453 "freeholders" owning more than 10 acres of land, and the 300 better-off Bridgetown householders, totals about 1,780.[22] Thus it appears that about two-thirds of the white population of the island were poor whites; and if the grand total for the white population of the island as a whole, estimated at 20,000, is reasonably accurate, this suggests a total of some 13,500 for the poor white section of the population.

The situation was evidently not a happy one. There was every encouragement for anyone who could leave to seek his fortune elsewhere. The effect of the gradual economic decline in the island, moreover, was greatly to reduce the possibilities of former indentured servants eking out some kind of existence. In 1661 the President, Council and Assembly of Barbados petitioned the Commissioners for Foreign Plantations, stating that sugar was so much reduced in value that many would have to quit the island unless their desires for increasing its value were met. These desires included the transportation of their produce in English bottoms to any friendly port. In 1663 the Governor, Francis, Lord Willoughby, informed the King that unless the restrictions imposed by the Navigation Acts could be removed, the colonies would all be ruined. As it was, some thousands had already left Barbados and the Leeward Islands for the French and Dutch colonies.[23]

Fortunately for the individuals concerned, there were various possibilities that were then opening up. People were still needed for Jamaica, and official pressure to encourage Barbadians to go there continued from some quarters. In London, the Council for Foreign Plantations noted that every opportunity should be taken to contribute to the defence, welfare or increase of Jamaica by allowing those who had been servants in Barbados to go there freely. This was reinforced by the arrival in Barbados in July 1662 of Lord Windsor, Governor of Jamaica, on a recruiting drive. Although he received somewhat limited support from the authorities in Barbados, Lord Windsor's declaration that those going to Jamaica would have allotments of land even if they were servants, that tradesmen would be encouraged, that there would be no religious coercion, and that there would be free commerce with foreigners evidently caused considerable numbers to leave Barbados for Jamaica. Further encouragement was given to this trend in 1664 by the removal of the eminent planter, Sir Thomas Modyford, to Jamaica on his appointment as Governor, accompanied by some eight hundred people,[24] and followed by a further two hundred or so in 1671.[25] One emigrant from Barbados, Henry Morgan, who had started life in the West Indies as an indentured servant, was to achieve prominence first as a pirate and later as Lieutenant Governor of Jamaica.[26]

Elsewhere in the Caribbean, Barbadians went to St. Lucia, where a group of a thousand settled there in 1663 by Francis, Lord Willoughby, was wiped out by the Caribs.[27] In the American Colonies, Barbadians also went to Carolina, following an officially inspired and locally supported initiative taken in 1663 by the Corporation of the Barbados Adventurers which envisaged the settlement there of "many hundreds of noble families and well experienced planters, that are ready to remove speedily thither, with negroes and servants."[28] The result was that South Carolina became a permanent settlement in 1670, though perhaps not quite on the scale originally envisaged. In any case, the number of white servants involved would not have been large.

In addition to those who left Barbados to settle elsewhere, a number left, many of them never to return, on military expeditions in connection with the Second and Third Dutch Wars (1664–67/1672–74) and subsequent attempts from Barbados to assert English sovereignty over islands in the Windwards and Leewards. Some eight hundred were involved in 1665 in actions against the Dutch in Tobago and Guiana, while another three thousand went on expeditions in 1660 in attempts to regain St. Kitts, and another seven hundred in the same year to various parts of the Leeward Islands.[29]

The available figures of immigration during these years are now so scanty as to make any estimate of the total number of immigrants out of the question. The lists drawn up at English ports in accordance with the regulations which came into force in 1664 are fragmentary and the information at the Barbados end of the pipeline almost nonexistent. Indeed, the Governor, Jonathon Atkins, was to state in his despatch on the census of 1680: "I can give no account of the people that arrive in the Colony; few white servants come."[30] The emigration figures, on the other hand, although only quoted in round figures, are such as to make some sort of very approximate estimate possible. According to one estimate, in the years 1660 to 1667 some ten thousand people, mainly landless freemen and small farmers, left Barbados, followed in 1668 to 1672 by four thousand to five thousand people, mainly of the planter class, and in 1678 to 1682 by another two thousand planters, giving a total of sixteen to seventeen thousand emigrants during those years.[31] Even if these figures are somewhat exaggerated they still represent a large scale movement out of Barbados, with many of those leaving being poor whites.

The population figures, although unlikely to be entirely accurate, and providing as a rule no breakdown of the white population into its various categories, nevertheless give an indication of the effect that these changes in the pattern of white migration, measured against the number of African slaves coming into the island, were having on the racial balance of the population. A very approximate estimate suggested for the white population of 20,000 by 1660 was probably just about equalled by the black population.[32] The first official census, taken in 1673, spoke of 21,309 whites and 33,184 blacks, with the latter figure being considered by the Deputy Governor to have been underestimated by one-third, which, if true, would have brought the ratio of blacks to whites to a little over 2:1.[33] The next official census, carried out by Governor Atkins in 1680, suggested a total white population of about 20,000, compared with 38,782 slaves. Governor Dutton's census of 1684 showed 19,568 whites and 46,602 "coloureds."[34] Thus the trend of a declining, or possibly a static white population, becoming rapidly outnumbered by a growing black population was already well established.

For almost the next thirty years there were no census returns or any other figures for which any accuracy was even claimed. In 1690 the Governor estimated the white population as twenty thousand and the black as six-hundred thousand—even if the latter is a mistake for sixty thousand, as seems likely, it indicates a significant intensification of the contemporary trend[35] (see Table 1). In 1697 an anonymous letter to the agents of Barbados lamenting the languishing state of the island referred to the number of white men as having sunk in twenty-five years from twenty thousand to three or four thousand.[36] While this clearly indicates some confusion between the total number of white people, including women and children, and the number of white men, it nevertheless suggests not only some actual diminution of the white population but a panic-stricken attitude to the whole matter of the racial balance, or imbalance, of the population.

Table 1. Population Figures 1660–1690

Year	Whites (total)	Poor Whites	Slaves	Total
1660	(20,000)		(20,000)	
1673	21,309		33,184	54,493
1680	(20,000)	?13,500	38,782	(58,782)
1684	19,568		46,602	66,070
1690	(20,000)		60,000	80,000

Sources: See notes to the text.
Note: Figures given by sources as estimates are in parentheses; figures estimated by the writer are indicated by a question mark.

It is small wonder that this situation was causing concern to the authorities. With the increase in the proportion of blacks to whites, the possibility of slave uprisings could be expected to increase and the capacity of the whites to deal with them to decrease. In fact, there were a number of serious alarms: in 1675 one conspiracy was discovered;[37] in 1686 investigations into a reported uprising of slaves in conjunction with white servants were carried out;[38] in 1692 a slave plot to massacre the whites, in which several Irish servants were alleged to have been involved, was uncovered;[39] and in 1701 plans for a slave mutiny and rebellion were suspected.[40]

At the same time, the danger of foreign invasion remained constant during this period of intermittent wars with the Dutch and the French. The inefficiency of the Militia, in which the bulk of the private soldiers was made up of servants and former servants, was glaringly obvious. It was reported in 1673 that the Militia consisted of two regiments of horse and six of foot, amounting to one thousand and four thousand men respectively, which comprised "the utmost number of white men capable of military service, so small are their numbers, and so infirm by age, sickness and personal defects (or mental, in which quality they deem the Quakers) are the rest; so are already enforced to arm part of their blackmen." By 1690 the Militia was said to be in a "lamentable state."[41]

This was clearly a situation in which drastic action was necessary if the island was not to be left vulnerable to both internal and external attack; the first line of defence was, then, to tap possible sources of supply in order to get more people to come to Barbados. William, Lord Willoughby, when he was appointed "Chiefe Governour of the Caribbee Islands" in 1667, was instructed to be "all ways encouraging the bringing in of Xtian Servants and Planters into these islands."[42] Evidently his predilection was for Scottish servants, who had indeed shown themselves to be the most satisfactory of the servants reaching the island, in contrast particularly to the Irish, who were always causing trouble in one way or another. Referring to servants from Scotland, he wrote shortly after his arrival in Barbados: "I wish more of them, the worst of whom would serve my turn, and live happily here, and do the King good service. Near on 4,000 servants would be upon honourable terms entertained; and if in my time they can be supplied this country would be willing to pay their passage." But he added: "We have more than a good many Irish amongst us, therefore I am for the downright Scot, who I am certaine, will fight without a crucifix about his neck."[43] After this, subsequent governors made repeated efforts up to the early 1690s to obtain servants from Scotland. Petitions, pleas, representations to the King, all containing accounts of the disastrous situation which would result if no more white servants reached Barbados, had no effect; no authority could be given to waive the requirements of the Navigation Acts, which effectively prevented Scottish ships from carrying servants to Barbados because they were not allowed to pick up any cargoes from the colonies for their return journeys.[44]

Then, in 1690, when all hope of getting servants from Scotland was being abandoned, the possibility of sending servants from Ireland was mooted. The Council of Barbados, nonetheless, in spite of the urgent and still largely unsatisfied need for white servants, continued to insist on servants from Scotland to strengthen the Militia, saying: "We desire no Irish Rebels may be sent us during the War; for we want not labourers of that Colour to work for us; but men in whom we may confide, to strengthen us."[45]

There appeared to be only two other possibilities. In 1697 the Council of Trade and Plantations, knowing only too well of Barbados' requirement for white servants, enquired about the possibility of the transportation of a number of malefactors in Newgate prison; Barbados proved to be the only place prepared to accept them, provided that women, children and infirm persons were excluded.[46] In the same year the possibility of resettling disbanded soldiers in the colonies was under discussion; Barbados was prepared to accept them under the conditions of an "Act to encourage the bringing in of Christian Servants to this Island" of 20 June 1696. The Act provided for the importer to receive the sum of eighteen pounds per servant and for persons transporting themselves to get the same amount, as well as for an increase in the existing allowance of flesh or fish to six pounds per week, a reasonable supply of clothing and wages of £1.5s.0d a year.[47] Apparently this latter scheme had some success; by the next year it was stated that "Considerable numbers of them have been Imported, and More daily expected to replenish our decayed Militia."[48] The problem now became one of placing these servants. A total of five laws passed between 18 May 1699 and 27 February 1700 laid obligations on various categories of persons to employ white servants and furnish them to the Militia and, finally, arranged for the disposal of such servants as might still remain once the requirements for the Militia had been met in full.[49]

Curiously enough, very little attention has been paid to this considerable later influx of white servants. The total number brought in under the terms of the Act of 1696 was assessed by the Agents of Barbados at over two thousand—nearly twice the number of regular indentured servants who had left Bristol for Barbados during the peak years 1655 to 1660. But in spite of the fact that extraordinary efforts had been made to acquire these servants, including their purchase at what was described as "an excessive charge," evidently no particular efforts were made to keep them in Barbados. They were expected, at the end of their periods of indenture, to go off "as is customary . . . to Pensilvania, Carelena, and other Northern Colonies where provisions are more plenty and weather more temperate."[50]

Thus the various measures which had been taken during this period to make living and working conditions for white indentured servants less unattractive had had very little effect; there was obviously no possibility of reestablishing the flow of regular, or indeed of any other type, of indentured servants. In fact, the first piece of legislation passed during this period, namely, the "Act for the good governing of Servants, and ordaining the rights between masters and servants" of 27 September 1661, had done very little to help in this direction, although it had admittedly shown at least the beginning of some concern for the well-being of servants. In the main this Act merely sought to consolidate existing legislation safeguarding the rights of masters, rather than to give any protection to servants, but it did include one interesting new provision. This was contained in clause 12:

> And whereas it is much feared, that some persons within this Island, have exerted violence and great oppression to, and upon their servants, through which some of them have been murdered and destroyed . . . Servants shall not be interred out of the usual burying place of the Plantation, nor till the bodies have been viewed by the next Justice, or a Constable and two Neighbours . . . If it appears that they came to their deaths by violence, the Viewers to give notice to the Coroner, who shall inspect the same.[51]

Thus, although the defence and internal security of the island pointed to the pressing need to encourage servants both to come to Barbados, and to stay once they had settled, the planters themselves showed few signs of taking any action to improve the conditions of their servants. Most unusual, therefore, were the instructions given about this time by Sir Henry Drax for the management of Drax Hall and Irish Hope Plantations. In them he stated unequivocally that "it will be necessary to encourage the white servants according to their Meets, either by an extraordinary Allowance of Cloathes or Provisions, or if you see cause, of some Wages."[52] Generally it was the governors, in the face of obstructions from the planters, who attempted to introduce legislation to prevent servants from being treated with cruelty. In 1681 Sir Richard Dutton, in a speech to the Assembly, advised that consideration be given to a law to restrain bad masters and overseers from cruelty to their Christian servants. On introducing the bill, however, he was informed by the Assembly that masters needed to be protected against malicious complaints as much as servants needed to be protected against severity.[53] Again, in 1691, a similar attempt by James Kendall was frustrated by the Assembly's comment that "they had perused the Laws between the Masters and Servants, which they found very full to prevent any cruelties or ill usage to be done them by their Masters."[54] Not until 1701 was there reference in any act to the method of obtaining redress in the event of severe usage by a master of a servant,[55] and not until 1703 did the Assembly, in considering and eventually passing further legislation of the same kind, agree "most heartily" with the Governor that there was a need for "effectively discouraging the ill usage of Christian servants."[56]

In any case, probably of more immediate and practical value in improving conditions was the legislation providing for specific quantities of meat or fish in the diet prescribed for servants. Although earlier indenture terms had included meat and drink "according to the custom of the country," there had obviously been a great lack of protein in the diet. In 1682, however, masters were required to provide servants with five pounds of flesh or fish per week as well as sufficient plantation provisions and clothing. In 1696, as has been noted, this was raised to six pounds and reiterated in 1701 as six pounds of "god wholsom and Sound flesh or fish per week," a provision also included in the Act of 1703,[57] which was the last one to be passed concerning the welfare of white servants.

The extent to which these regulations were observed was, of course, another matter. In 1695, more than ten years after the provision for five pounds of fish or flesh had been made, the Governor, referring to the condition of the hundreds of white servants "who never have a bit of fresh meat bestowed on them nor a dram of rum" and who were "domineered over and used like dogs," made an interesting, if somewhat unorthodox, suggestion. This was that the suffrage should be extended to all those possessing two acres of land and forty shillings a year, so that candidates for the Assembly, to which elections at that time were held annually, would "sometimes give the poor creatures a little rum and fresh provisions . . . in the hopes of getting their votes."[58]

There were, however, even more fundamental causes of dissatisfaction which were to have very serious repercussions over the next two centuries. One of these was the long-standing problem of the lack of land. One suggestion, made in 1666 by the Lieutenant Governor, was that out of every one hundred acres of land belonging to the rich, ten should be given to the poor. Action of this kind was hardly likely to appeal to the planters, but their awareness of the size of the problem may be gauged by the fact that even the Gentlemen Planters in England, a group of influential but mainly absentee landlords, included, in important proposals put to the authorities in Barbados in 1670, a suggestion about the restriction of property, with the object of keeping up the number of freeholders. This suggestion was that no one in Barbados already possessing land should be allowed to purchase more. It was modified the next year, making it more acceptable both to the landlords and the local planters, by a recommendation that no one possessed of twenty-five acres of land should be permitted to buy, rent or receive more except by inheritance.[59]

The Gentlemen Planters' other proposals concerned the substitution of locally produced cloth for the fabrics imported from France and Germany for the clothing of servants and slaves, and the restriction of the employment of blacks on specialised work, or trades, to that of artificers in sugar works on the plantations to which they belonged.[60] These two restrictions were in their way perhaps as important as the one concerning the restriction of land. The idea of encouraging the cotton industry was a practical one—cotton was rated second only to sugar in a list of commodities reported by the Governor as late as 1676[61]—and was to recur from time to time throughout the years without ever being seriously put into practice. The significance of the substitution of slaves for ex-servants in the various specialised tasks on the plantations as a contributory cause in the deterioration of the poor whites' condition has already been noted, and was to be repeated later in varying forms.

This initiative on the part of that very powerful group of planters resulted in the passing, on 4 June 1671, of an "Act to prevent depopulation." The preamble stated the immediate problem clearly: "Whereas the safety and prosperity of this island next to the blessing and protection of Almighty God doth depend on the numbers and strength of Christian inhabitants who on all occasions will doubtless prove themselves most serviceable and ready both in resisting foreign invasion and also putting a stop to intestine insurrection . . . ." It then went on to deal with two of the matters about which representations had already been made. On the question of land it did not provide for any limitation of ownership, as had been suggested, but it did introduce two measures designed to improve the position of the landless freeman. One was intended to encourage large plantation owners to rent land to poor householders for the purpose of farming. The other provided for the rating of two tenants, with leases of at least three years on plots of two acres of land, as the equivalent for Militia purposes of three freemen or servants. On the point regarding the unemployment of white men resulting from the employment of slaves in specialist jobs on the plantation, it stipulated that plantation owners were obliged to employ one qualified white man for each slave engaged in a specific trade. Similarly, people in towns had to employ one Christian man or boy for every black man or boy working for them.[62]

According to the covering letter with which the Assembly sent a copy of this Act to the Gentlemen Planters of Barbados in London, its purpose was to encourage poor freeholders and to deter covetous men from laying land to land without keeping up cottages and families. There was no reference to the point about the employment of white men; this may well have been accepted from the start as quite impossible to implement. There was also a reference to a separate Act encouraging the manufacture of cotton,[63] but this Act does not appear to have reached the statute book.

While the intentions of the legislators may have been good, this Act appears to have achieved very little. It was repealed in 1688 on the grounds that some clauses were covered in other legislation, some unnecessary and others contradictory.[64] The problem of the lack of land was, of course, quite insoluble without measures of so extreme a kind as to be quite inconceivable at this time. The creation of the "military tenants," which provided a short-term solution by making land available to some of the landless freemen in exchange for their service in the Militia, was incorporated into the Militia Law and was to lead a century and a half later, after Emancipation, to a new wave of unemployment among poor whites. The provision for matching each slave artisan with a white man with similar qualifications passed rapidly into limbo. By 1697 a further and more drastic suggestion for restricting the employment of slaves was made with the proposal that they should be used only for work in the fields, leaving domestic service and the trades to whites.[65] Predictably, this also came to nothing.

It was thus that the efforts of forty-odd years had been in vain. All the attempts to avert the decline in the white population had failed; even those who had been persuaded by one means or another to come to Barbados found conditions such that they moved on at the earliest opportunity. Much more serious, however, in the longer term, was the total lack of success in laying a secure foundation for the descendants of these indentured servants, who were destined therefore, for many years to come, to remain trapped in the condition of poor whites.

Chapter 4
From Indentured Servants to Poor Whites
(1704–1839)

In retrospect it seems a blessing that the measures of the latter part of the seventeenth century to bring in white servants had so limited and short-lived a success. It was, however, by no means clear either at the time or for some years to come. For at least the first four decades of the eighteenth century, public bodies and private individuals in London as well as Barbados, when not preoccupied with problems of dealing with unsatisfactory governors, were most concerned with the declining fortunes of the island. They continued to believe that a solution might somehow be found by keeping up the level of the white population. But judging by the almost complete lack of any contemporary comment on the situation of the former indentured servants, they failed totally to realise that they were in effect conniving at the emergence of a class of poor whites which was to pose serious social and economic problems for Barbados in the very near future.

The first census of the century, taken in 1712, gave a total of 12,528 white inhabitants, compared with 41,970 slaves.[1] The figure for the whites, however, seems likely to be an underestimate when it is compared with the figure given in the more detailed census of three years later, though it confirms in no uncertain terms previous indications of a considerable drop in the proportion of whites to blacks. This evidently caused some concern in London and resulted in the Council of Trade and Plantations asking the Governor, in July 1715, for information on the decrease in the number of men able to bear arms, and for an investigation into the legislation concerning the number of white men which planters were obliged to keep on their estates. This was followed a fortnight later by a request for proposals for the better peopling and settling of Barbados.[2] This initiative resulted in the production of a complete list of all the white inhabitants by name, totalling 16,888, but offering little else, except for some interesting details of liaisons between whites and mulattos in the parish of St. Philip.[3] On the point concerning legislation, the Governor stated that he believed that many of the planters did not have the required number of servants and that he would keep the matter under review.[4] Indeed, the Militia Act of 1697 had provided, with certain qualifications, for planters to provide one man for the Militia for every twenty acres of land held, but it had stated also that persons should not be penalised for failing to send the required number of men.[5] With the continuing decline in the white population, it was unlikely that by 1715 the planters were anywhere nearer meeting their quotas nor, however much the Governor might review the situation, was there anything very much that could be done about it.

Nearly twenty years later a new Governor, Lord Howe, raised the question of the depopulation of whites again, in the context of the impossibility of the island's undertaking any responsibilities for defence, and thus inspired an enquiry by a committee of the Privy Council into the decrease of white men in the British West Indian islands. Based on the findings of this enquiry, the Council of Trade and Plantations explained the situation as due to the low price of sugar in England and the resulting decline in trade, the departure of people for places of greater security, the non-observance of the laws obliging landowners to keep a certain number of white servants in proportion to their slaves, the training of slaves for trades and for shipping, and the tendency of the rich to engross land and thus force the poor to go abroad.[6] These thoughts were not new—they contained unmistakable echoes of the recommendations of the Gentlemen Planters a half century earlier. At the same time, the misconception on the matter of the proportion of white servants to slaves should have been removed some years before when the agents for Barbados had informed the Council for Trade and Plantations that there was no legislation of this kind in existence and, as far as they could ascertain, neither had there ever been.[7] Once more, no action was taken. Again, in 1738, after Lord Howe's death, the President of the Council of Barbados, James Dottin, expressed the view that the place was so depopulated and the planters had so little to lose, that resistance to an enemy might not be adequate and that if Barbados was worth keeping it must therefore have a guard of warships.[8]

By the middle of the century all hope of reversing the decline in the white population had evidently been abandoned. With 15,252 whites and 47,025 blacks in 1748, the ratio of blacks to whites was over 3:1; this was to climb by 1768 to over 4:1 and by 1829 to nearly 6:1[9] (see Table 2). Immigration, whether voluntary or forced, had by this point virtually ceased. Between the years 1718 and 1759, according to the Guildhall lists, only 39 persons left London for Barbados compared with 3117 going mainly to America and Jamaica.[10] Between 1719 and 1744 only eight of the criminals being transported to the colonies were sent to Barbados, compared with 7,275 bound mainly for Virginia and Maryland.[11] It was only that most valuable source of labour which had been exploited a century earlier by Cromwell that made any noticeable contribution to the reinforcement of the white population in Barbados, namely, the despatch to Barbados of a group of 150 Highlanders taken prisoner during the Jacobite rebellion of 1745, 127 of whom appear to have eventually reached Barbados. The Highlanders had pleaded guilty to the crime of high treason but had been granted a free pardon provided they indentured themselves to serve in the colonies in America for the term "of their Natural Lives." This period was defined as seven years, after which they might be released from their servitude on condition that they remained permanently in the colonies.[12]

Table 2. Population Figures 1712–1834

Year	Whites (total)	Poor Whites	Slaves	Free Coloureds	Total
1712	12,528		41,970		54,498
1715	16,888				
1748	15,252		47,025	107	62,324
1768	16,139		66,379	448	82,966
1829	14,959		82,902	5,146	103,007
1834	12,797	(8,000)	82,850	5,584	101,231

Sources: See notes to the text.
Note: Figure given within parentheses is an estimate.

Meanwhile, emigration continued apace from Barbados to the colonies elsewhere in the West Indies as well as in America. John Poyer, the Barbadian historian, writing anonymously at the time to the new Governor, Lord Seaforth, in 1801, regarded the emigration of the "lower classes of People" as disastrous, saying: "thus the strength of the country is diminished, and the Common Stock deprived of a due proportion of Labour and Industry." Poyer also blamed the exodus on the lack of encouragement given to the white mechanic as well as the practice of using the slaves as "tradesmen."[13] This had been a cause of concern from as early as the mid-seventeenth century since it was seen as the means whereby former indentured servants were deprived of their traditional modes of employment.

It would be a mistake, however, to regard the plantations as having been totally denuded of white servants. The accounts of Lowther's plantation for the year 1756, for example, include references to servants' wages for the manager, driver and bookkeeper as well as the housekeeper and others engaged in more menial tasks.[14] That this was still the normal practice is confirmed by a treatise published at about the same time which recommended that a plantation of five hundred acres should have a house for servants and a staff of six, ranging from the chief overseer down to a white groom and herdsman.[15] Indeed, an "Act concerning white servants" passed in 1755 provided for the prosecution of servants employed "by Covenant,

Indenture or Contract in writing" who were absent from their posts, without due cause, for more than forty-eight hours.[16] As late as 1786, a set of instructions for the management of plantations drawn up by a group of planters laid down that white servants should have a "proper apartment to live in ... (and) a proper cook to dress their victuals" which should be "the best which the country affords to this class of men and served to them in a decent and cleanly manner." In addition, the chief manager was to enforce the observance of strict order and decorum among the white servants, to prohibit all improper intercourse between them and the slaves, but yet to "temper his discipline with kindness."[17]

Nevertheless, there were indubitably fewer white persons employed on the plantations than previously. One writer stated in 1755 that, whereas in earlier years several planters had had from twenty to forty white servants, of late years very few had more than four white men on their plantations, all the labour being performed by slaves.[18] The occasional white men would thus, to an ever increasing extent, occupy only the most senior positions. It is no doubt for this reason that, from about the middle of the eighteenth century, there is a tendency for the terms "servants" and "freemen" to be replaced in official documents by "poor whites." The majority of the former white servants were being forced to seek employment outside the plantations and failed to make an adequate livelihood.

Some of the former servants continued, as they had previously, to acquire land and cultivate it, usually with the help of a slave or two. Others worked the plots they held by virtue of their service in the Militia. Those who had trades were sometimes able, though to a decreasing extent, to practice them. Many subsisted by fishing, or by keeping little retail shops. Those who operated as hucksters faced severe competition, as in other spheres, from the free coloureds. An attempt made in the Assembly in the 1770s to introduce legislation to preserve this occupation for the whites by obliging the free coloureds to buy licences, was frustrated when the Act was eventually passed in 1779 with provision for licences to be obtained by hucksters of all shades.[19] Poor white women in the country evidently tended to work alongside the men on their plots and to carry the produce to market.[20] Some of the women were employed also on the plantations in making clothes for slaves,[21] though sewing for the planters' families was normally done by the house slaves. Others worked as domestics, though this latter work was unpopular.

There are indications that the ranks of the poor white women were swollen by the addition of some who were of rather superior status to the average poor white person. In 1818, in connection with a proposal to carry out a large scale campaign to provide some basic education for the slaves, it was suggested that poor white women might be used for teaching, since "the country abounds in poor white women, many of whom, not altogether incapable of such an undertaking, might be induced to engage in it, on the prospect of proper encouragement."[22] That nothing came of this is indicated in the only available document providing what purports to be a first-hand account of the life of a poor white. This is a letter quoted in a weekly newspaper column by the "Prattler" as coming from one who signed herself Jane Aimgood. After having received some education from a relative who took her into her house on the death of her parents, she became employed as a housekeeper. In one case she was obliged to leave her employment because of unwelcome attentions paid her by the master of the house; in another case she suffered from the extreme meanness of her employers; in a third case she was ridiculed by the slaves in the household; and in a fourth case she was suspected by her mistress of conniving at the licentious behaviour of her husband. She also described how at one time she had been a companion to a relative as poor as herself and how they had kept themselves from starving by needlework even though "the needle is a scanty resource for indigent white females, and yet it is the only one they have." She finally expressed the wish that something might be done "to soften the unhappy state of the poor white women of this Island."[23]

One practical attempt to improve the situation of the poor whites was that made by the legendary Joshua Steele, author of *Prosodia Rationalis* (1779), and sometime Vice-President of the Royal Society of Arts in London. Steele had arrived in Barbados under somewhat questionable circumstances in 1780 to take over a plantation which he had inherited from his wife's former husband. He busied himself with attempts to reform the system of slavery on his own plantation, much to the dismay of his fellow planters, and also with trying to devise methods of encouraging cottage-type industries among the poor whites in an attempt to persuade them to abandon their idle and dissolute ways. To this end he formed a Society for the Encouragement of the Arts, Manufactures and Commerce in Barbados, which, among other things, drew up a plan for developing small-scale manufacturing enterprises, particularly for the spinning, weaving and dyeing of local materials.

The Society succeeded in getting a bill through the Assembly providing for the local vestries to obtain and store supplies of tools and materials and to hand them out to poor manufacturers on repayment at a later date out of the proceeds of their work. It was hoped that this would promote industry among the "Poor Artisans, who, where such favourable Helps are wanting, are unable to exert the Faculties of which they are possessed, and may then resign themselves in this soft Climate to the Pleasures of Indolence, although connected with the Discomforts of Beggary."[24] The bill was passed in January 1783, and, if subsequent developments in the parish of St. Michael repeated themselves elsewhere, it had very little in the way of positive results. There the vestry decided to give the scheme a trial run and voted the sum of seventy-five pounds for the purpose. Inquiries five months later into the progress of the operation revealed that little or no work had been done and most of the money remained unspent; the fifty pounds that was left over was to be used for repairs to the almshouse.[25]

This lack of enthusiasm may well have been due in large part to the sceptical attitude of the planters towards Steele's various schemes. In any event, the Society lasted less than ten years without having had any enduring impact. In 1857 the editor of the *Barbadian*, referring to pamphlets that he had received from the Royal Society of Arts in London, stated that he had no knowledge of the earlier existence of any such society in Barbados, and commented that he did not think that there was scope for such an organisation there "with its limited and already developed resources."[26]

The poor whites, at this stage, were not only an embarrassment to the plantocracy and a burden to themselves, but they were also facing greater competition from the free coloureds. The latter were becoming an increasingly important section of the population and had reached over five thousand by 1829.[27] The Archdeacon of Barbados stated the position unambiguously in an appendix to the published sermons he had delivered at the Cathedral in 1833 on the subject of "Christianity and Slavery":

> The free blacks have, by their superior industry, driven the lower order of whites from almost every trade requiring skill and continuing exertion. I believe that not one in twenty of the working shoemakers in Barbados is a white man. The working carpenters, masons, tailors, smiths etc. are for the most part men of colour; and this at a time when a large white population are in the lowest state of poverty and wretchedness.[28]

This was obviously not a situation making for a satisfactory relationship between the various classes of society. Indications have already been given of the disinclination of the planters to concern themselves with the welfare of the poor whites, to whom they naturally regarded themselves as immensely superior. The poor whites, in their turn, considered themselves to be far above the slaves and were thus determined to maintain this position by refusing to degrade themselves, as they saw it, by doing the same kinds of work as the slaves. But now they were confronted by a new breed of people, not white, but yet free, and evidently far more competent than they at doing very much the same types of jobs as those which they had long regarded as their prerogative. This, then, gave rise to considerable animosity between the two groups of poor whites and free coloureds.

Joshua Steele's friend and colleague, William Dickson, had drawn attention in no uncertain terms, and with the use of vivid examples, to the fundamental belief of the poor white that he was in every way the superior of the Negro;[29] the facts of their situation at the end of the eighteenth century ought to have made them question this belief, but their ignorance, being what it was, merely served to increase the resentment. Indeed, this reached such a point that, in 1799, in a memorial from the free coloureds to the Governor in connection with the discharge of a white man who had been indicted at the Court of Grand Sessions for the murder of a free coloured man, it was stated: "many profligate white persons have threatened to kill some of your Memorialists without the slightest provocation; and we not only walk abroad under apprehension of being assassinated, but we are continually in dread of being murdered in our houses."[30]

That this fear was not without justification was attested to a few years later by the Governor, Lord Seaforth, when he was in the process of conducting a campaign not only to bring about some improvement in the state of the police, but also to have legislation passed which would have made the murder of a slave a felony. He found that "to the greatest remissness in the execution of the Laws is joined the most barbarous and insulting oppression of the Blacks and coloured people by the refuse of the whites," and he cited three cases of "horrid murders" selected from a large number of similar ones. In all the three incidents poor whites—a Militia man, a plantation manager, and a butcher—had murdered slaves, two of them women and one a youth, in circumstances of extreme brutality.[31]

The comparative condition of the poor white in relation to that of the black, whether slave or free, had been receiving attention in a number of quarters for some time. A physician, Richard Towne, was perhaps the first writer formally to draw the comparison to the attention of the public, though he did so perhaps inadvertently, in a treatise on local diseases published in 1726 after he had spent some seven years in the island. He noted, in a chapter on diarrhoea, that "fluxes" were common in the rainy season among "Negroes and the poorer sort of white People who in these seasons are much more afflicted with this Distemper than such whose condition of life does not subject them to such inconveniences." Dysentery was stated to rage "among the White Servants as well as the Negroes on the Plantations, which sort of people are much addicted to debauch in Spirits, and Punch made exceeding strong with new Rum, very acid with Juice of Limes, and very fermentative with coarse sugar." He also found that elephantiasis, which he claimed did not exist in Europe, nevertheless in Barbados affected "white people whose unhappy circumstances have reduced them to hardships but little inferior to what the Blacks are obliged to undergo."[32] These findings were later quoted by the Reverend Griffith Hughes in his *Natural History of Barbados* published in 1750.[33] The doctor and the parson were to a large extent responsible for sparking discussion and comment on the situation of the poor whites in relation to the blacks which, while throwing useful light on the position of the former, seems at the same time to have provoked much hostile comment.

The controversial question of the effect of a tropical climate on the European constitution was also one of the subjects that was batted back and forth during this debate; it even received some attention in official quarters in Barbados towards the end of the century when the future likely effects of the emancipation of the slaves were being discussed. A questionnaire, relating mainly to the conditions of slaves but including some items referring to poor whites, elicited the reply from members of the Council, in answer to one question dealing with the suitability of the European for field work on the plantation, that there had been "no single instance of a European dedicating himself to anything like hard labour in exposing himself to the sun who had been able to support the heat of this climate; nor do we think it possible."[34] The Governor, David Parry, was evidently not entirely satisfied with the results of this questionnaire and put further questions to Joshua Steele, who replied to a question on the effects of the climate thus: "although the climate is remarkably salutary, both to black and white, under equal treatment, the probability seems to be, that it should be more suitable to black workers in general; and yet white labourers are found to bear the hardest labour that is necessary, without any inconvenience, until they destroy their constitutions by rum-drinking and venery."[35] William Dickson commented to the same effect, noting that Barbados had originally been cultivated by whites and he saw no reason why "temperate, seasoned white men" should not work on the plantations in the same way that they cultivated their own private plots of land without any assistance from Negroes.[36]

The debate was continued by two early nineteenth-century visitors to Barbados. One of them considered that the physical appearance of the poor whites indicated that the climate was "irreconcilable with the condition of the race."[37] The other, a medical doctor, evidently agreed with Dickson's view that there was no reason why European labourers should no longer be able to withstand the climate and went on to imply that the reason for their apparent inability to do so was their general attitude toward work: "there is no lack of inhabitants in Barbados of the labouring classes—I beg their pardon, of the poorer classes, for labour is a disgrace for a white man in all slave countries, which the poorest wretch is ashamed to submit to."[38] Indeed, various comments made from the turn of the century suggest that the poor whites were in a state of serious physical and psychological deterioration. It was at this time that the term "Redleg," or sometimes "Redshank," appears to have come generally into use. Dr. Williamson's reference to the "Redlegs" as gaunt in appearance, arrogant by nature and generally useless and degenerate, was earlier noted. The comments on the "Redshanks," made in the *Yarn of a Yankee Privateer* had also emphasized their arrogance, together with their idleness and degradation. J. B. Colthurst's remarks about the "Redshanks" in the Militia further confirmed these impressions.[39]

Indeed, the very appearance of these people was evidently such as to provoke a reaction not only from the foreigner describing his impressions of an unfamiliar country, but also from a Barbadian writing of his familiar native land. The poet H. J. Chapman enquired at the time:

> Who are those wretches of the lead-like hue,
> That seem some plague-ship's horror-haunted crew—
> Those nerveless children, woebegone and pale,
> Whose limbs seem wire-hung, and whose sinews fail?[40]

Commentators were again struck by the juxtaposition of the poor white and the black population. A doctor, who, as Deputy Inspector General of Hospitals to His Majesty's Forces, spent three months in Barbados in early 1796, referred to the existence of "a poorer order of white people ... who obtain a scanty living by cultivating a small patch of earth .... They are descended from European settlers, but from misfortune, or misconduct in some of the race, are reduced to a state far removed from independence; often, indeed, but little superior to the condition of the free negroes." Somewhat curiously for a man who presumably had had some scientific training, he also expressed surprise that, although they had been in Barbados for generations and had been exposed to the same life and work as the Negroes, they had remained entirely European in their physical character-istics.[41] Traveller H. N. Coleridge commented after his visit in 1825: "many of the wretched white creoles live on the charity of the slaves, and few people would institute a comparison on the respectability of the two classes. The lower whites of that island are without exception the most degraded, worthless, hopeless race I have ever met with in my life. They are more pressing subjects for legislation than the slaves, were they ten times enslaved."[42]

Perhaps the clearest picture, though one marred, inevitably, by moral judgements, was provided by a young man of eighteen years who was living in Barbados in the 1820s with his father, who was in the Army:

> Of all the classes of people who inhabit Bridgetown, the poor whites are the lowest and most degraded: residing in the meanest hovels, they pay no attention either to neatness in their dwellings or cleanliness in their persons; and they subsist too often, to their shame let it be spoken, on the kindness and charity of slaves. I have never seen a more sallow, dirty, ill looking and unhappy race; the men lazy, the women disgusting; and the children neglected: all without any notion of principle, morality or religion; forming a melancholy picture of living misery; and a strong contrast with the general appearance of happiness depicted on the countenances of the free black, and coloured people, of the same class.[43]

With Emancipation the number of observers coming to the West Indies inevitably increased, and while investigating the effects of Emancipation on the former slaves, they could not fail when in Barbados to notice the situation of the poor whites. Their comments on the "Redshanks" were generally in line with those of earlier visitors. They were particularly struck, as one would expect at this juncture, by the contrast between the blacks and the poor whites and the obvious inferiority of the latter. One of the reports highlighted the salient features of the poor whites: "many . . . are dependent on parochial and casual relief, and even on the charity of the apprentices. The competition of the coloured people has driven them out of almost every field where free labourers were wont to exercise their skill and industry. From their idle and dissolute habits they are more degraded than the negroes, but are proud of their caste as whites."[44]

Only one visitor to Barbados during these years saw the situation differently. Dr. Thomas Rolph, who was in Barbados in 1833, saw the poor white inhabitants as "objects of the raillery and vituperation of those flippant writers who have adopted the opinions of others," and he castigated Coleridge in particular. Rolph claimed to have made himself thoroughly familiar with all the features, including the social conditions, of the island, and he commented on the poor whites:

> I found them, in industrious habits, respectful demeanour, becoming attire, and sobriety, fully equal to any white man, in the same rank and station in life. In all their habitations, and patches of land which they cultivate, he might have discovered the effect of industrious and well regulated inhabitants. And it is a matter of great astonishment that they are enabled to work under a vertical sun, the thermometer frequently standing at 90° in the shade, and manage to cultivate their ground and raise ginger, arrowroot, cotton, aloes and cassava, breeding poultry, and produce stock for sale.[45]

It was little wonder, given contemporary notions of racial superiority and of what was considered also to be the appropriate relationship between coloniser and colonised, that the majority of foreign observers experienced a kind of "culture shock" at seeing white people living at a similar, or sometimes even inferior, level to black people. It was unfortunate, in the interests of putting the situation in perspective, that apparently none of them thought it worth relating the conditions they observed in Barbados to those obtaining in the England, or indeed, the United States of the time. Had they done so, they would have had to acknowledge that the living conditions of the poorest classes in their big cities, while not dissimilar in terms of over-crowdedness and squalor, were in fact markedly worse than those of the poor whites in Barbados. The latter at least enjoyed certain compensations by virtue of the climate. Nevertheless, provided one discounts the highly charged emotional language in which some of these comments were made, the sum of their findings, when examined in conjunction with local comments and actions, shows the appearances of authenticity. Dr. Rolph remains the one exception in this extensive collection of observers.

In fact, the overdramatic nature of some of the published comments may well have been of some value in opening the eyes of local people, whether private citizens or officials, to a situation in which action was obviously necessary, even if only on humanitarian grounds. The "Prattler," for example, writing in 1822 not only about poor white women but about poor whites generally, admitted their unhappy plight, blaming it at least to some extent on the "moral system" of the island, in which the relationship between master and slave was of prime importance, and which he held responsible for the growth of false pride. This resulted in the poor regarding work as degrading, although, as he said somewhat smugly, "we all know that honest employment is virtue, and idleness is vice."[46] More practical, though not fundamentally dissimilar, was the assessment contained in a report produced in 1836 to inform the Secretary of State for the Colonies in England of the workings of the post-Emancipation system. This referred to the situation whereby the poor whites regarded both field and domestic labour as degrading, and it drew attention to the fact that in Bridgetown the "free blacks and persons of colour have nearly supplanted the whites, in almost every trade; the consequence is that the lower class of whites are in a state of degeneration and destitution."[47] Thus, even in Barbados, people had begun to realise that some kind of action would have to be taken. In fact, from the last quarter of the eighteenth century a number of measures were introduced both to alleviate the immediate distress and to initiate longer term action to improve the position of the poor whites.

Officially, responsibility for poor relief lay with the vestries of the various parishes, which also carried out the responsibilities of local government. References are to be found dating back to the 1650s to the provision of pensions for certain poor people in the parish of St. John,[48] and there is no reason to doubt that the same pattern would have been followed in other parishes. Private individuals had also concerned themselves with this problem. Richard Carpenter in 1662 had bequeathed four thousand pounds of Muscovado sugar annually to be used for the poor of St. Philip,[49] a bequest which interestingly is still in operation today, thus providing a curious example of a direct link with the hard days of the former indentured servants. An Act of 1675 referred to a legacy from a Mr. Philip Trowel "for or towards the Support or Maintenance of Five poor decayed English Men" in the parish of Christ Church, and in 1681 no fewer than eight legacies which were to be used for the poor were listed in the parish of St. John.[50]

The vestry system of poor relief, however, was inadequate at the best of times and had to be supplemented by the Government in periods of exceptional hardship. A petition which was sent to the King in 1776 drawing attention to the possibility of famine due to crop failure and the embargo on trade with North America showed serious concern for the situation of the poor whites. The petition itself included a reference to "the extreme difficulty with which our numerous poor white inhabitants support themselves and families," and a covering letter from the speaker, Sir John Gay Alleyne, contained a most graphic description of their plight: "those in the neighbourhood of the coast come down to it, in small flocks, to gather the most wretched of all the fruits of the earth to eat for their subsistence, and when the ripe ones were all gathered, they then gathered the green ones to boil, and therebye soften them, as food to keep their lives and souls together."[51] Again, in 1797, a long drought had brought about a situation in which the importation of provisions from America was "absolutely essential to the preservation of the properties and lives of the inhabitants, particularly the poorer order of the whites and the numerous body of slaves."[52] In 1812 another long drought was causing distress among the poor whites, particularly those who, as billeted men and tenants, formed part of the Militia. Some of these were stated to have "often felt the pangs of hunger ... subsisting for days on very little, or scarcely any kind of solid food whatever"; eventually £3,000 was voted for their relief and this was increased a few weeks later in view of the "present dreadful scarcity of food being particularly hard on the lower classes of people."[53] In 1826 a further sum of money was granted towards the relief of the poor of the parish of St. Philip.[54]

In addition to these government measures, private organisations were formed in the first half of the nineteenth century in an attempt to do something to help the poor. The Ladies' Association for the Relief of the Indigent Poor and Infirm, founded in 1825, ran a Daily Meal Dispensary and an Asylum in Bridgetown; the former by 1835 provided just under a hundred meals a day for all poor people, irrespective of colour, and the latter housed a dozen or so poor white women. A clothing club was formed in the parish of St. Michael in the 1830s, and in 1839 a start was made in improving medical services for the poor when a public meeting was held to discuss the erection of a general hospital to be maintained by voluntary contributions.[55]

Early attempts were also made in the sphere of education to supplement the very limited schooling the vestries were able to provide for the children of the poor. Already in the seventeenth century bequests had been made to found three schools. In the parish of St. Peter, in a will made in 1679, Peter Hancock left his house and land to provide a free school "for the Teaching and instructing of ... the Sons of poor Parents, in Grammar and the knowledge of the Latin Tongue etc. and for the maintenance of the said poor scholars and their Master," and even stipulated that the pupils should "weare Coates of gray Sarge or stuff all of one fashion and make."[56] The school, if indeed it ever came into existence, seems to have been short-lived, for early in the next century the house was in a state of decay.[57] Henry Drax, in 1682, also left £2,000 to endow a free school in Bridgetown; there was apparently at least a schoolhouse in existence in 1696 when some French prisoners were accommodated there, but it seems to have lapsed after that. Again, in the 1680s, three bequests in St. George should have insured the maintenance of a school on the Bulkeley estate, but it evidently soon fell into disuse.[58]

In spite of this early lack of success, the first half of the eighteenth century saw some concern being shown over the lack of educational opportunities.

The Grand Jury, in its Presentments for the years 1705, 1707 and 1719, had referred to the need for schools for the poor, recommending that the free schools already founded should be finished, and that the use of donations for the education of youth be investigated in view of the "want of publick schools for the education of youth being in great measure the cause of the present corruption of manners."[59]

These representations appear to have had some success, though, in one case at least, it was short lived. In 1708 whatever was left of the free school in St. George was to have been repaired and used as a school, but by 1711 it was again in need of repair since it had been used as a prison and by the 1730s it was once more out of use with the result that in 1737 the church warden was to consult the Attorney General about the recovery of the Bulkeley grant.[60] Another bequest, which was made in 1709 by Francis Williams, seems not to have had any results for a century. In 1733 Harrison's Free School was opened to provide education for not more than twenty-five poor and indigent boys from the parish of St. Michael. It had, however, from the start also taken fee-paying pupils, and though it continued to give free education to its foundation scholars,[61] it could not be regarded strictly as a school for poor whites. In 1745 the Society for the Propagation of the Gospel started Codrington Grammar School with seventeen foundation scholars, four of whom were orphans and one the son of a servant. All students were to be the sons of poor persons of good character who would not otherwise be able to educate their children. This school, later to become the Lodge School, also had fee-paying boarders from the start,[62] and although for a time it carried out the dual role of a charity school and grammar school, by 1813 it had abandoned its former role and admitted only the sons of gentlemen.[63]

The next seventy-five years saw the opening of three more schools, all of which were concerned with the education of poor white children. In 1785 the Seminary in St. Andrew, endowed by Sir John Gay Alleyne, opened its doors to pupils.[64] In 1809 Francis Williams' bequest bore fruit when the first foundation stone was laid of the Foundation School in Christ Church, which was to provide education for the poor children of the parish.[65] In 1819 the Central Schools were founded in Bridgetown for the purpose of educating boys and girls from all over the island.[66] The schools had started with voluntary contributions but from 1822 they received a government grant of eighty-eight pounds a year; the original Act specified that there were to be twenty-six boarders, who should not be under eight or over fourteen years old.[67] In addition, some training in practical crafts, such as spinning and knitting, was provided for girls by the School of Female Industry in St. John, which was in existence from 1792 for some fifteen years.[68]

While these schools appear from contemporary accounts to have been reasonably efficient, they provided education for only a small proportion of the poor white population; the rest of the poor white children were receiving such education as they could get from parish resources, which were generally totally inadequate, and which sometimes did not run to anything approaching schools in the formal sense of the word. There were, according to Bishop Coleridge, only six church schools for poor whites in existence in 1825,[69] though they were extended to the other parishes within the next few years. In the parish of St. Philip in 1808, for example, children were frequently put out to be schooled by a variety of totally unqualified persons; the building of schools, however, was under consideration in 1832 and the schools began operating the next year with twenty-nine boys and twenty-five girls.[70]

Another important point in considering the state of the educational system at the time was the capacity of the children, many of whom were living in conditions of extreme poverty, to benefit by such teaching as was available. In St. Joseph, in 1839, a vestryman, writing to the press concerning the need for proper school buildings stated: "the poor white children have been to a miserable hovel near the ruins of the old church, and when they do attend school, it is a day to many of them of starvation. This is a fact. Their destitution is incomparably worse than that of any black or coloured children in the Parish."[71] Indeed, this recognition of the plight of the children was no doubt responsible for the practice which was generally in operation in the schools, whether parochial or otherwise, designated for poor white children, though not, apparently, in St. Joseph, of providing meals, clothing and sometimes boarding facilities.

The necessity, if education was to be of any help in improving the situation of the poor whites, of providing not only suitable instruction in practical subjects but also help in obtaining situations and some kind of continuing supervision, was in the minds of some of those concerned with these problems in the early years of the nineteenth century. A committee appointed by the vestry of St. Philip in 1808 to enquire into the state of the poor included in their report not only recommendations for more adequate schooling but also for insuring that no pupil left school without being found a position as an apprentice, and, since master workmen preferred the more hard-working black apprentices, for giving premiums of ten pounds with each white child bound as an apprentice.[72]

Of particular interest for its comments on the educational system generally, its past and present defects and its recommendations for the future, which concentrated very much on the need for practical training, was a treatise written in 1827 by J. W. Orderson, sometime editor of the *Barbados Mercury*. He referred to the lamentable degeneracy which prevailed among the lower classes of white people, in contrast, once again, to the coloured population, and blamed this largely on a defective educational system. This, he wrote, had caused children to be thrown on society with "scarce more than a smattering of reading and the first rudiments of arithmetic, and with all the predominant indiscretions of vulgar juvenility" and the result was that soon after they left school "all trace of them is lost in those active and useful pursuits which the coloured people have usurped and now successfully rival them in; while they . . . associate themselves in profligacy and vice with the already initiated, and for a precarious existence, become gamblers, cockfighters, runaway catchers, thieftakers and informers; in short, sink into the mere dregs of the community."

His close examination of the annual reports of the Central Schools suggested to him that insufficient attention was devoted in the curriculum to practical work and that there was inadequate provision for supervising pupils once they had left school. His very detailed recommendations included instruction in such trades and crafts for boys as carpentry, joinery, bricklaying, shoemaking, saddlery and book-binding; and in domestic subjects and knitting, spinning and weaving, particularly in local materials, for the girls. He appealed, finally, to the ladies of Barbados to set up a Society for the Promotion and Encouragement of Arts, Manufactures and General Industry with the aim, among others, of generally inducing habits of thrift, cleanliness and economy among the lower classes.[73]

It is impossible to estimate accurately the proportion of poor whites in the total white population of 14,959 at the time of the 1829 census. One assessment, made shortly after Emancipation, when the total white population was 12,797, placed the number at about 8,000,[74] but this figure may have been rather low (see Table 2). In any case, the problem facing the authorities was a sizable one, and, as has been seen, none of the initiatives taken during that period seemed likely to get at its root, namely, the inbred resistance of the poor whites to working at the same types of jobs as people of the same social level but of a different colour. The severe repercussions on the poor whites of the growth of the free coloured population were multiplied many times with Emancipation in 1834 and, more particularly, with the end of the apprenticeship system in 1838. At this stage vastly more black persons were seeking employment and thus competing with the poor whites, and almost always to the disadvantage of the latter. The situation was further exacerbated with the reorganisation of the Militia in 1839 which, as will shortly be seen, threw some two thousand poor whites, formerly living on the estates as military tenants, on to the labour market without either the will or the capacity to find employment which would give them an adequate livelihood.

Chapter 5
Disbandment of the Military Tenants (1839)

While the years from the 1660s to Emancipation in 1834 saw a gradual erosion in the position of the former indentured servants as they were largely replaced in their traditional occupations on the plantations by the slaves, and later on in their artisans' jobs in the towns by the growing population of free coloureds, there was one sphere in which they enjoyed a virtual monopoly. This was the Militia, which from the early days of English settlement had played an important role in Barbados on account of its dual function as both an internal security as well as an external defence force. As was inevitable, it was exclusively composed in the early days of members of the white population. The planters occupied the positions of officers, holding their commissions through their property qualifications. Small freeholders, freemen and servants, whether indentured or free, formed the rank and file; from 1671, however, freemen without land could acquire plots of land on a lease hold basis in exchange for their services.

The Carlisle/Courteen controversy of the first two years of settlement, which had involved some fighting, marked the beginnings of the establishment of a Militia. Under Philip Bell's governorship from 1641 to 1650, the reorganisation of the Militia was undertaken on rather more formal lines than had been the case hitherto. Legislation at that time provided for the settling of "trained bands" and of a regiment of horse, and, by March 1650, of a "standing force," with appropriate measures for the supply of arms and ammunition. An Act which was evidently passed near the beginning of this period concerned the "encouragement of servants to defence, in case of invasions."[1] By the time Ligon left Barbados in mid-1650 he reckoned that the Militia consisted of "ten thousand Foot, as good men, and as resolute as any in the world, and a thousand good Horse."[2] Though Ligon's figures may be exaggerated, the existence of a strong Militia was of considerable importance when the uneasy truce between the Cavaliers and Roundheads in Barbados broke out into armed hostility. When a force headed by Sir George Ayscue was on its way to Barbados to put an end to its near independence,

57

and ensure its submission to the Commonwealth of England, Francis, Lord Willoughby, Lieutenant Governor of the Caribbee Islands, was able to raise an army of six thousand foot and four hundred horse in an attempt to prevent its landing.[3] In spite of Willoughby's action, however, when he "kept the field at the head of his brave Militia, composed principally of the common people,"[4] the Barbadians eventually signed an agreement, on 11 January 1652, acknowledging the authority of the Commonwealth.

One of the results of the political settlement was a further reorganisation of the Militia. Property qualifications were laid down for officers, ranging from one hundred acres for field officers down to fifteen acres for ensigns, and making an exception so that substantial merchants might have commands where appropriate. Regulations were drawn up concerning the liability of landowners to provide men and horses; they had to send one able man, provided with a musket and ammunition, for every twenty acres, and one able man and a horse for every hundred acres. In addition, service in the Militia was made to apply to a wider range of persons by requiring all freemen, including householders, labourers or artificers to provide themselves with muskets and join the Militia, and by requiring all freemen with horses to serve. Encouragement was given to indentured servants by promising them remission of half their time if they conducted themselves manfully in any engagement with an enemy.[5] At this stage the Militia consisted of five infantry regiments of one thousand each and a troop of four hundred horses.[6]

During the next fifteen years, the strength of the Militia remained somewhere between five and six thousand.[7] Nevertheless, even if the numbers remained constant, there were evidently serious inadequacies in the standards of performance, which were highlighted by the need to improve the defences of the island with the outbreak of the Second Dutch War in 1665. In 1666 a proclamation was issued by the Governor that two "suitable Negroes" should accompany each trooper on alarms.[8] This did not, of course, imply that slaves would become formal members of the Militia which, as was clear from the Militia laws, was restricted to freemen and white servants. It seems, nevertheless, a somewhat surprising move in the light of the subsequent slave conspiracies, and presumably one dictated by expediency. It was interpreted some years later as a move necessitated by the generally decrepit state of the white men forming the Militia.[9] At the same time, the shortage of white servants available for Militia service was by then becoming obvious to the authorities; indeed, the lack of any regular paid force was commented on adversely by an observer in the late 1660s.[10] However, although some legislative action was taken during these years, no significant change was to be made in the conditions of service in the Militia until the 1670s.[11]

As has already been seen, one of the most important factors in discouraging servants from coming to Barbados, and also encouraging them to leave once their periods of indenture were over, was the shortage of land. They received none by way of recompense for their services, and rents and prices generally were too high for them to pay. The Act to Prevent Depopulation, passed on 14 June 1671, was intended to build up the numbers and strength of the "Christian inhabitants" of the island for the purpose of internal and external defence, and it sought to do this by encouraging landowners to make small plots available to those serving in the ranks of the Militia by providing that "at all musters and exercises ... every two tenants appearing in arms for the landlord shall henceforth be taken and deemed equal to three common free men or servants, and considered always that every such tenant that occupy or possess two acres or more of land they have a lease of the same for three years at the least."[12] This provision was probably incorporated into the Act for the Settlement of the Militia of this Island of 14 March 1672;[13] it certainly appeared in the Act with the same title of 15 April 1680 which reiterated that service in the Militia was compulsory for "every freeholder, householder, artificer, labourer or other freeman."[14]

This attempt to solve two different though related problems, namely, the encouragement of former servants to remain in the island and the putting of the Militia on a sounder basis, not only failed in the short term but also was to have very serious repercussions in the future. As far as the Militia was concerned, the provision for military tenants evidently did not make up for the overall deficiency in the numbers of the rank and file; efforts to remedy this were to continue for some years. The Militia Act of 3 November 1697 provided for the remission of statutory punishments for landowners not sending the required number of people to the Militia, on the grounds that it was unfair to punish people for impossibilities as long as they sent all the tenants and servants they had or could procure. It also sought to give further encouragement to servants by providing for the complete remission of their remaining periods of indenture in the event of their satisfactory fight against the enemy, and to make up for deficiencies by providing for apprentices and others unable to provide military equipment for themselves to be billeted on landed men.[15] The success which was achieved, at great expense, in getting some two thousand men to come to Barbados in the late 1690s seems to have had only a temporary success in filling the ranks of the Militia since most of these men left, at the end of their periods of indenture, for more salubrious climes.

Not even the impetus provided by the various slave conspiracies of the last quarter of the seventeenth century, nor by the wars with the French and the Dutch, seems to have resulted in any improvement in the Militia. By 1703 the new Governor, Sir Bevill Granville, was writing to the Earl of Nottingham that he found the "fortifications bad and in very ill order, the militia which is its best strength by sickness and the difficulty of getting white servants from Europe lessen'd to a degree very unequall to what the defence of it requires."[16] The only real innovation during this period had been the creation of the system of military tenants, but even this proved unsuccessful, whether from the reluctance of the landlords to grant leases or the disinclination of

the former servants to engage in agricultural work, even on their own be-
half, or from a combination of the two. Perhaps its most important result
was in the encouragement of a section of the poor white community to regard
itself as particularly privileged.

Until 1795 virtually no legislative action was taken to improve the unsatisfactory state of the Militia. The internal security situation, admittedly, was
reasonably quiescent. An incident that occurred in 1761, in which acting
attorneys on a plantation in Christ Church parish encouraged armed blacks to
obstruct bailiffs in the course of trying to execute writs, was regarded rather
seriously by the Council in view of the encouragement it might give to
others,[18] but it appears to have been an isolated case. Externally, however,
Barbados remained subject to intermittent threats of war with France, which
turned to fact with the outbreak of the Seven Years' War in 1756, the French
seizure of Dominica in 1778, and the French declaration of war against
England and Holland in 1793, which precipitated action uncomfortably
nearby in the islands of Grenada, St. Vincent and St. Lucia.

Nevertheless, such action as was taken with regard to the Militia appears to
have been restricted to sporadic and evidently unenthusiastic attempts to see
that the provisions of the existing law were complied with, particularly as far
as the responsibilities of the planters to provide the stipulated number of men
were concerned.[19] It was not that the need for action was not recognised;
there seems to have been no doubt in anyone's mind, from the Governor on
down, that the organisation of the Militia was generally unsatisfactory and the
law defective. There was, however, considerable resistance to the idea of the
Militia being reorganised on an efficient basis, possibly on account of fears
that this might concentrate too much power in the hands of one individual.[20]
The authorities evidently preferred to deal on an ad hoc basis with each
emergency, even when amounting to the possibility of an invasion, rather
than reorganise the Militia in such a way that it would constitute a significant defence force. As for the men, although the military tenants naturally
were expected to meet their obligations, the rest of the poor whites had no
intention of carrying out any military duties which they could possibly avoid.
In considering the possibility of raising troops locally in 1794, the Assembly
dismissed as impracticable a proposal to raise five-hundred white Barbadian
troops since such were "the dispositions of the Poor White People . . . that . . .
no premium, no Temptation, would induce one hundred to enlist."[21]

The report of a committee of Joshua Steele's Society of Arts provides the
most valuable single account of the Militia in relation to the rest of the
community during this period. The committee had been set up early in 1783
in order to consider, in general, the extent to which the Militia law was
injurious to the community and, in particular, whether the system of military
tenants was such a burden to the estates, and provided such encouragement
to the poor to seek parochial aid, as to counterbalance its usefulness in
providing a military force. The ensuing report put into words much of the
feeling which had caused resentment throughout the years, namely, that the

Militia was a waste of time. It found that the law was in fact injurious to the island in that it dislocated the work of the plantations by taking people away on unnecessary marches in response to needless alarms. While admitting that the system of military tenants helped to keep up the number of white people in the population, it nonetheless severely criticized it as being counter-productive in that it put an unnecessary burden on the landowner and encouraged tenants in habits of idleness and vagrancy, which were also proving a serious problem to the parish authorities.[22]

The latter point was taken up by a committee of the Assembly which reported in 1787. It suggested that three useful purposes might be served by making the military leases terminable: tenants would be encouraged to work; they would carry out their service in the Militia better; and, in addition, the cultivation of small plots of land which would otherwise be wasted would be achieved. This committee also made an important suggestion to the effect that all fines for non-compliance with the law should be imposed on a sliding scale so that they fell more heavily on the rich than the poor.[23]

When the new law was eventually passed, on 7 January 1795, it introduced what was regarded as a more equitable system by requiring all freemen from seventeen to sixty to serve. The freemen would, of course, include a proportion of the free coloured population, which by this time totalled some two thousand.[24] It also reduced the number of men to be sent by landowners to one for every forty acres, and provided for houseowners to send one man for every house of the yearly rentable value of eighty pounds. The position with regard to tenants remained fundamentally unchanged, except that the acreage requirement was increased so that each man counted as sixty acres. A graded system of fines was laid down according to property qualifications.[25] A subsequent law, passed on 4 December 1799, reduced the acreage to thirty, with a tenant counting as fifty acres, thus increasing the number of men to be made available. It also made an attempt to keep up the required numbers for each plantation by providing for billeted men to be transferred from adjacent parishes where necessary.[26]

During the years between the passing of this Act and Emancipation, there were a variety of minor changes in the law but no major revision. This period was marked by two episodes of some significance for the Militia. One was the threat in 1805 of invasion from the French, which precipitated the passing of a temporary Act to call out the Militia.[27] The other was the slave insurrection of 1816, which caused the Militia to be brought into action, and resulted in the successful quelling of the rebellion. It is interesting to note that the free coloureds were reckoned to have conducted themselves "slightly better" than the poor whites during these encounters, which fact was to be used later that same year to support a bill designed to remove the disability of the former with regard to the giving of evidence.[28]

The Act for the Abolition of Slavery throughout the British Colonies received the royal assent on 28 August 1833 and was to come into effect on 1

August 1834. Only persons of outstanding breadth of vision could have begun to imagine the repercussions which this event would have throughout the British West Indies as well as elsewhere, but even the Barbadian authorities, who were not generally renowned for their flexibility, had to start to adjust to the radically changed condition of society. One of the most urgent needs, other than those of meeting the requirements of the Abolition Act itself, was to change the pattern of the Militia. This had previously been based on the principle that every free man was bound to serve, which would clearly no longer be appropriate when all men were free.

The first attempt to draft a new Militia bill ran into difficulties, but a revised bill eventually received the Governor's assent, and none too soon, on 29 July 1834. It entirely changed the basis for service in the Militia by restricting obligation to serve to those possessing at least five acres of land, a house of the yearly rental value of twenty pounds, employment as an attorney or manager, or in any other job at a minimum salary of twenty pounds a year; it continued to include tenants and billeted men on the same terms as before.[29] The latter two categories would thus comprise the only persons serving who would be an exception to the property or employment qualifications.

This Act evidently did not meet the changed situation adequately and a new bill was introduced in late 1837 which sought to rationalise the system of qualifications in a more appropriate manner and, as part of this process, to abolish the system of military tenants, which had clearly become an anachronism. The bill ran into difficulties at all stages. When it was passed, on 4 December 1838, it made specific provision for the exemption from service of "domestic or menial servants, or Agricultural labourers,"[30] categories in which, at that time, almost all the former slaves would find themselves. This definition of service, however, met with strong disapproval from the Colonial Office in England, which suspended proceedings in connection with the Militia on the ground that, while it need not be disbanded if that were too repugnant, some method had to be found of recruiting without making distinctions of colour and class. Disbandment evidently proved to be too repugnant to the Barbadian authorities, and thus a new Act was passed on 13 August 1839 omitting the offending words and defining the property and employment qualifications in slightly wider terms than before.[31]

The matter of the disposal of the military tenants had met with some difficulties locally although its significance was not perceived by the Colonial Office. In the debate on the bill, opposition had been expressed to abolishing the system on the grounds of humanity, and comment at a later date indicated that the House of Assembly's "intentions were benevolent though severe; wishing to raise their character in the side of true respectability by obliging them to habits of honest industry in place of indolence and sloth."[32] In fact the Act provided for the tenants to be permitted to remain on the estates under the same conditions as before until January 1840; there was no further reference to billeted men and therefore that institution must be assumed to have been abolished without comment.

Thus, at the stroke of a pen, a considerable number of poor whites were both rendered homeless and deprived of the land which for many families must have provided their only means of support. They also lost the patronage which they would, in some cases at least, have enjoyed from their landlords. As the St. Philip vestry records show, when a sum of 250 pounds was granted out of parochial funds to buy supplies to help in rebuilding the houses of the poor after the storm of 1819, it was specifically stated that it was not to be used for the tenantry, who, it was presumed, would "receive every possible relief and assistance ... from their landlords."[33]

The people who formed this group were certainly not likely to be in any position to fend for themselves when deprived of their already much under-utilised means of livelihood. Commentators in the previous century had drawn attention in unambiguous terms to the physical and psychological deficiencies of the poor whites generally and there is no reason to think that this criticism did not include the holders of the military tenancies. Indeed, this was borne out in the comments made by the Society of Arts in 1783 in connection with the proposed Militia bill, to the effect that the institution of military tenants encouraged them in habits of idleness and vagrancy. In the early years of the nineteenth century in the parish of St. Philip, and probably in others, the vestry had on its lists of pensioners receiving poor relief a number of military tenants,[34] who, if they had cultivated their plots properly, should normally have been in a position to provide at least a modest living for themselves and their families.

The military tenants were to show no improvement during the few years immediately preceding their disbandment. J. B. Colthurst noted in his diary the uselessness of the Militia generally, castigating this "corps of Redshanks ... who are a nuisance to the Colony, and ... are ... profoundly ignorant, both of their religious and moral duties, and the most presuming set of rascals possible to conceive of." He also gave a visual record of a military tenant in his watercolour of "Sergeant Redshanks," which he emphasized, was not a caricature. He goes on to describe the scene: "The Sergeant often passes my door, urging on his starved beast as described, with his black girl hanging onto his horse's tail, as is usual up Hill and accoutred as shewn .... The Sergeant and his girl, now his apprentice—she of course is his maid of all work as well as attending him to muster and parade without his Breeches, his firelock, his belts, pouch and Plumed Cap—to dress on the field!!"[35]

Estimates of the numbers of military tenants, the proportion they formed of the total poor white population, and the proportion the latter formed of the total white population, are impossible to make now with any degree of accuracy. The total white population was given as 12,797 in 1834;[36] a year or two later the total poor white population was guessed to be around 8,000;[37] and the number quoted as having been thrown off the estates as a result of the 1839 Act was about 2,000,[38] which presumably referred to the men only and not to their families. Therefore it seems likely that something over half the total poor white population would have been affected by the terms of the new Act.

What, in retrospect, is surprising is that so little regard was paid at the time to the possible results of this action. It is true that the authorities must have been very much preoccupied with the various administrative and social implications of Emancipation, and perhaps the fate of two thousand or so poor white families was rightly considered to be of relatively little account compared with the adjustments which had to be made to accommodate over eighty thousand former slaves in the society. Nevertheless, the speaker in the debate on the 1838 bill quoted above, while evincing some concern, revealed small knowledge of the capacity of the average poor white of that time if he really thought that depriving them of their means of livelihood would have been likely to bring about a change of heart in them and turn them from indolent and slothful creatures into industrious citizens. Perhaps most revealing of all for lack of any understanding were those comments made on the Act of 1838 by the Attorney General, who, in speaking about the tenants, noted that provision had been made "to prevent the injury which might happen ... by too sudden a dissolution of their connection with their landlords," and by the Governor, who considered that the act would "relieve the poorer ranks in general, of whatever complexion, Whites included ... from the execution of an onerous obligation, by conferring on them ... the privilege of exemption."[39]

The first truly realistic comment on the situation of the military tenants appeared in March 1839 in the newspaper *Liberal,* edited by Samuel Jackman Prescod, the leader of the free coloured community, and later a member of the Assembly and a renowned judge. He published a letter purporting to be from a "Labouring Man" which referred to the poverty of those who had become tenants at the will and pleasure of their landlords and which called attention to the effects of the climate on these same tenants:

> I said you could not stand hoe work in this climate; and if you
> could, and were as constantly exposed to the sun as the field
> labourers are, why what a pretty set of boys you would be in a
> short time. Does not the heat of the Sun blister your nose, and
> draw up your lips, and disfigure your countenance, and
> enervate your frame? and have you not degenerated, and are
> you not degenerating from the form and figure of your
> European bretheren? Look at your children, see their parched
> faces.[40]

The only solution that the writer had to offer was that of emigration, in which he said the estate owners should be asked to help.

The implications of the 1839 legislation for this section of the population

West Indies—Barbados Militia Sergeant Redshanks Moving to Muster *(By courtesy of the Boston Public Library, Rare Books and Mss. Department)*

were to become manifestly clear during the remainder of the nineteenth century. Their situation was remarked upon frequently, not only by visitors of all kinds to the island but also by the Barbadian authorities, and additional measures to those inadequate ones which had been in operation since the end of the eighteenth century were gradually, and belatedly, introduced.

Chapter 6
The Problem of Degeneration

The passing of the Militia Act of 1839 without any serious legislative consideration of its probable repercussions was to receive almost continuous comment throughout the remainder of the century. A letter to the press written the year after the exodus of the military tenants and their families had taken place referred to the "abominable Act by which the poor whites were driven, like so many dogs, with their wives and children, from their tenements," and its author asked for someone to come forward to provide assistance for "our wretched and despised white peasantry."[1] Dr. John Davy, who, as Inspector General of Army Hospitals spent the years 1845 to 1848 in Barbados, and was regarded by Samuel Jackman Prescod as being someone who could generally be relied on as an impartial witness,[2] attributed many of the signs of physical and moral, and possibly intellectual degeneration, observed in the poor whites to the circumstances in which they found themselves. He noted that the position many of them had held as military tenants had vested them with a certain importance in the society enabling them to support themselves and their families with little exertion; thus they had acquired habits of idleness which were to blame for their present miserable condition.[3] This point, it will be recalled, had been made more than half a century earlier by the committee of Joshua Steele's Society of Arts that had been set up to report on the existing Militia system. Later in the century, a very comprehensive report was issued by the Commission on Poor Relief and commented thus on the situation of the poor whites:

> Their condition is a truly deplorable one, as they were until emancipation an important class in the community, legislated for and provided for to a considerable extent as the Militia of the island: but since that great social revolution, no longer required for that purpose and either unwilling or unable to adapt themselves to altered circumstances; while the efforts made to assist them ... have failed to arrest their rapid

downward progress into destitution and degradation.[4]

The military tenants had not, however, made up the whole of the poor white population. There were other poor whites living in the urban district of Bridgetown and in the rural areas, particularly on the eastern side of the island. Emancipation inevitably had its impact on them, too. Opinions canvassed in 1858 as to its effects on the poor whites generally varied considerably. Some observers took the view that it had on the whole had a beneficial effect in that they no longer occupied a privileged position, forcing them to depend on their own resources with, in the main, good results. In particular, it was said the removal of the stigma from field labour had induced some of them to work as agricultural labourers with others taking jobs as grooms, carters and herdsmen. Other commentators considered that it had caused considerable hardship through the cutting up of small holdings which the poor whites had previously cultivated with the help of one or two slaves, with the consequent absorption of these holdings into estates or their sale in small lots to the emancipated slaves.[5] Indeed, the poor whites were seriously affected by this redistribution of land. A petition in 1860 to the Christ Church vestry refers to "the Middle Class of Society ... from which Managers, Bookkeepers and Working Men are recruited" as having been almost annihilated as a result of the Emancipation Act; it goes on to say that "nineteen out of twenty of these small landowners are in the most abject circumstances and in many cases their homes have changed hands, while they fight to obtain the bread by which they subsist."[6]

As for the total number of poor whites at this time, it seems that the figure of 8,000 suggested in 1837 was probably too low. In the absence, however, of any statistics and, indeed, of any precise definition of poor white, it is futile to attempt any guesses. The impression, for it is no more than that, provided by Dr. Davy seems likely to be the nearest that one can get to accuracy. He referred to the whites as being divided into two classes: "the poor labouring portion of them, constituting the majority, and the smaller portion of those in easy or affluent circumstances."[7] With a white population given in the census of 1851 as 15,824, this suggests a figure of around 10,000 poor whites, using the term fairly broadly, which is not inconsistent with other evidence available.

It seems possible that Dr. Davy, who was referring to the period some ten years after Emancipation, included in his "poor labouring population" a section of the white population whose situation had worsened during those years, and who, while not in the usual sense of the term poor whites, could not have been regarded, by any stretch of the imagination, as living "in easy or affluent circumstances." These persons would have been members of the planter class who had gone down in the world. A reference was made in a newspaper article in 1841 drawing attention to the sad condition not only of the poor whites but also of those other whites "who have seen better days, who have moved in comparative affluence, (and) are suffering the extreme of want, but the world knows it not."[8] Many of these "new" poor whites were "decayed gentlewomen," of whom, it was stated in 1875, there were to be found "so many up and down the country."[9] By the time the Poor Relief Commission reported in 1878, this class of "poor gentlefolk" was described as being very large, consisting of persons originally well off, who "from adverse circumstances, had fallen from the higher sphere which they occupied ... into utter indigence."

However, while the main trend in social mobility in the white section of the population at this time was generally downward, there were some instances of upward mobility. Dr. Davy admitted that "instances occur from time to time of individuals, who by their intelligence, activity and good conduct, better their condition, and raise themselves into the aristocracy of the island."[10]

Thus, although the proportion of poor whites seems likely to have amounted to possibly two-thirds of the total white population in the immediate post-Emancipation period, the pattern was nonetheless starting to change. Governor Rawson, in his comparison of the census results of 1871 with those of 1851, referred to the serious effects of the cholera epidemic of 1854 on the poorest of the poor whites in the Scotland district, but ascribed the slight reduction in the white population between 1861 and 1871 chiefly to the decrease in the class of poor whites, particularly through emigration. He went on to state that such members of this group of former military tenants as had neither emigrated nor found employment had become "unfitted for employment on the estates, have sunk in the social scale—are living for the greater part in poverty and squalor—are known by the name of 'Poor Whites,' or in Scotland by that of 'Redlegs,' and are gradually disappearing as a class."[11] Though Rawson was, of course, inaccurate in suggesting that the former military tenants made up the entire class of poor whites, he was quite right, if somewhat premature, in his assessment of its gradual disappearance. The trend was certainly well established by the 1870s and was to continue to an increasing extent as the emigration of poor whites received a modicum of official encouragement and support during the next four decades or so.

In spite of Rawson's oversimplification of the situation, the effect of the disbandment of the military tenants in hastening the decline of this class as a whole was fundamental. An important feature of this event, with its partial severing of the links of the poor whites with the plantation system, was the gradual move it initiated away from the rural parishes of the southwest and central portions of the island and towards the east coast. At the time of Emancipation there had been poor whites not only in Bridgetown and in the Scotland district but also, by virtue of their Militia functions, in all the rural parishes of the island. Confirmation of this could be found in the existence, at that time, of parochial schools restricted to poor white children in all parishes except St. James and St. Thomas, where the schools, probably due more to the small size of the white population than to any progressive attitude on the part of the vestries, were open to all classes.[12]

By the late 1840s, according to Dr. Davy, the poor whites were located mainly in the Scotland district and in the poorer areas of the parishes of St. Lucy and St. Philip.[13] The census figures for the years 1851, 1861 and 1871, however, do not bear this out, though the lack of differentiation between poor whites and other whites makes any assessment somewhat uncertain. What is clear is that in the years 1861 to 1871, when the total white population remained almost stationary at just above 16,000, the rural parishes showed slight decreases in their white population, except for St. John which showed a considerable increase, and St. Andrew, St. Joseph and St. James which showed small increases. After 1871 all parishes, with the exception of St. Andrew, which had increased its white population negligibly by 1881, conformed to the general pattern of decline in which the total white population decreased from 16,232 in 1871 to 12,063 in 1911[14] (see Table 3).

Table 3. White Population by Parishes 1851–1911

Parishes	1851	1861	1871	1881	1891	1911
Bridgetown	3,336	2,868	3,125	3,782	3,336	2,701
St. Michael	1,977	3,209	2,998	3,201	3,646	3,309
Christ Church	1,568	1,686	1,625	1,593	1,483	1,579
St. George	940	901	762	751	694	411
St. Philip	1,572	1,544	1,515	1,385	1,301	891
St. John	1,117	1,099	1,243	1,160	1,170	788
St. James	666	622	671	588	486	304
St. Thomas	577	525	499	449	394	290
St. Joseph	1,109	1,017	1,066	1,008	995	595
St. Andrew	834	832	860	864	774	398
St. Peter	1,219	1,120	1,115	949	825	494
St. Lucy	909	784	753	600	509	303
Total	15,824	16,207	16,232	15,780	15,613	12,063
Poor White	(10,000)					

Source: Official census reports.
Note: The figure in parentheses is an estimate by the writer.

The increase in the white population of the eastern parishes at the expense of the other rural parishes should not, however, be regarded as indicating a wholesale exodus of poor whites to that side of the island. A somewhat incomplete poor relief summary for the years 1870 to 1874 showed poor whites still receiving aid from the vestries in St. Lucy, St. Peter, St. Philip and St. Thomas. The remaining rural parishes, St. George and St. James, give no breakdown as to the complexion of the persons receiving poor relief,[15] but St. George had a school providing education in 1874 for twenty-seven poor white children.[16] Nevertheless, the move towards the east coast which had previously been to some extent the preserve of poor whites, where the climate was likely to be more agreeable to people originally from the British Isles, and, more importantly, where there were marginal lands available at lower rents than was the case elsewhere, was already well established by the end of the nineteenth century.

Inevitably, owing to their previous involvement in the plantation system, the majority of poor whites were not fitted for any occupation other than agricultural work, and even for this they were not too well equipped. They preferred, however, to do it, if at all possible, on their own account. Dr. Davy noted:

> Those who possess a little land or who rent a few acres, cultivate chiefly those crops which require least labour and the smallest means, such as ground provisions, arrowroot, aloes, and perhaps a little cotton . . . . Some who have been taught to read and write are engaged as book-keepers by the proprietors of the larger estates . . . . Some gain livelihood as carters and grooms and some as field labourers, a kind of occupation which, when slaves only were employed in field labour, would have been resisted by them as an insupportable degradation, and even now is only engaged in from necessity, and with good reason, for they are ill-fitted for much work.[17]

Work in the fields had in fact been so unusual for any white person that a commission investigating the state of agriculture in 1838 drew particular attention to an incident which had taken place in St. Joseph, where four poor white men had offered their services as day labourers on an estate. This event was reported as significant in that it might well open the way to an improvement in the situation of the poor whites.[18] Poor whites were certainly now prepared, if absolutely necessary, to work in the fields. Schomburgk remarked that "as land became so much more valuable after the emancipation, many were now obliged to work with hoe and bill on the sugar plantations, and many a white face may now be seen among the negroes labouring in the fields."[19] In St. John, for example, poor whites were reported in 1878 to work "very willingly" as field labourers on two estates, Clifton Hall and Newcastle,[20] and as late as 1914 and 1915 visitors noted that white labourers were still occasionally to be seen working in the fields.[21]

Fishermen in the Parish of St. Philip *(By courtesy of the Barbados Department of Archives)*

The view of the Poor Relief Commission, however, echoed the opinion expressed earlier by Dr. Davy: poor whites were regarded as being not only physically unfit for the labour of digging cane holes, but also as lacking in sufficient energy to be useful in any other departments of agriculture. During the course of the century they had evidently tended to drop out of the semiskilled jobs on the plantations. One witness called by the Commission reported that fifteen years previously all the boiling house and mill hands on his estate had been white whereas by the 1870s there were only two or three whites so employed. In the opinion of the Commission, the poor whites were generally too proud and prejudiced to work in the same industries and on the same level as people of colour.

One rural occupation in which they engaged, presumably because, although it could be hard work, it was on an individual basis, was fishing. Dr. Davy noted that "some are chiefly occupied in fishing, and that of a simple kind, by means of the casting net, and are to be seen exercising their skill on the shore, almost among the breakers, apparently at risk of their lives."[22] This seems to have become a traditional pursuit for poor whites. An opinion was even expressed on one occasion at a Christ Church vestry discussion that secondary education for poor white boys would not be valued by them and as soon as they left the school instead of following some useful occupation they would turn fishermen or butchers."[23] Indeed, as late as 1905 or 1906, a photograph of a group of nine fishermen in the parish of St. Philip showed at least five of them to be unmistakably white men.[24]

There were, admittedly, some new possibilities of employment that had begun opening up for poor whites at this period. One of these was the police force, which had been expanded immediately after Emancipation, and which welcomed poor whites into its ranks. J. B. Colthurst, concerned during his two years in Barbados with the organisation and training of a small body of police officers, made reference not only to their poverty, which had initially caused them to join the police, but also to their presumptuousness in considering their entry into the force as "conferring a favour on the public at large." Thus, they insisted on having grooms to deal with their horses rather than carrying out these duties themselves.[25]

New opportunities were also presenting themselves in the expanding commercial sector of Bridgetown, where the mainly white-owned firms preferred to employ whites. As one mid-nineteenth century traveller to Barbados remarked: "none of these people rise above the third class in England, all being shopkeepers, shopmen, and clerks to the various merchants, and, as might be imagined, the general level of society is very low."[26]

There was also a tendency among poor whites to become butchers, as has already been seen, and this was confirmed by a newspaper comment which indicated the derisive attitude of upper-class whites not only toward the occupation but also toward the class of persons engaged in it: "we have been requested to notice the very reprehensible conduct of certain butchers, we believe of the most vulgar class (though they have white skins, and may fancy themselves on that account a superior order of beings) who, on Saturdays when the market place ... is crowded with people, amuse themselves with pelting persons who are buying and selling, with cattle hoofs etc. etc."[27]

Women, particularly, continued to experience difficulty in finding work. With Emancipation there was no more employment for them on the plantations in making clothes for slaves; and they refused to work as domestic servants, regarding this as beneath them,[28] so that by the 1870s many of them evidently had to turn to prostitution as a means of earning a living.[29]

In discussing the types of work undertaken by the poor whites, it must be borne in mind that, with the increased strain on the labour market in the post-Emancipation period, unemployment was the rule rather than the exception. While this was not always the case, the negative attitude of the poor whites towards work runs like a thread through all the comments written in nineteenth century references to the poor whites. Schomburgk stated that the majority of them consisted of a class "*sui generis*; too proud to earn their living by manual labour, they were too poor to carry on the cultivation of the staple articles on their own account."[30] A traveller a few years later, noting their idleness, disclosed that "work is the detestation, the *summum nadum* of these creatures."[31] Though these observers, like earlier ones, were probably to some extent the victims of culture shock, there can be no doubt that the poor whites were caught in the grip of a downward spiral composed of the two strands of incapacity and arrogance and possessed neither the intelligence nor the energy to reverse the trend. There seemed no prospect for them other than that of a continuing decline.

The poverty in this section of the population was most certainly extreme. Even those who had their own plots of land must have lived at subsistence level with little or no margin to utilize when natural disaster struck or when ill health or family crises arose. The situation appears to have been particularly bad in the 1840s as a result in large part of the dispossession of the military tenants. There were reports in those years of poor whites dying of starvation and of a worsening of their situation with the drought of 1847. Cases were cited in the press of all the children in a parish school but one having left home in the morning without a morsel of food, and of poor families, even those possessing five acres of land, being in a state of actual starvation with no food on their land and no money to buy any.[32] The situation was evidently so bad that the vestries' resources were unable to cope and the Government had to be brought in. Loans were granted to supplement the funds available in the parishes of St. Joseph and St. Philip, which evidently had been hardest hit in the drought.[33]

An analysis of the figures of poor relief for the years 1870 to 1874 reveals that, in the six parishes for which adequate figures are given, almost $4\frac{1}{2}$ percent of the total white population were recipients of poor relief —compared with just over 1 percent of the total black population. This figure does not take into account the parish of St. Joseph, where many poor whites lived, since no figures for St. Joseph were given. It was stated, however, that poor whites formed a majority among the overall total of people receiving poor relief.[34]

One of the factors which made the poor whites virtually incapable of hard work was certainly their physical degeneration. Dr. Davy's description of the typical poor white's appearance suggested that this was the case:

> Their hue and complexion are not such as might be expected, their colour resembles more that of the Albino than that of the Englishman when exposed a great deal to the sun in a tropical climate; it is commonly of sickly white, or light red, not often of a healthy brown; and they have generally light eyes and light coloured sparse hair. In make they bear marks of feebleness, slender and rather tall, loosely jointed, with little muscular development. In brief their general appearance denotes degeneracy of corporal frame, and reminds one of exotic plants vegetating in an uncongenial soil and climate.[35]

Another visitor to Barbados, in 1844, had described their figures as "mean and attenuated."[36] A later observer, in 1895, described a white overseer, mounted on a "sorry nag," wearing a mask over the lower part of his face in accordance with the "custom in this island," since white people working in the fields found that "their lips are apt to blister, and after a time to fall back from the teeth; the face becoming scarred as if from a burn."[37]

The extent to which these physical traits were the result of the conditions in which the poor whites had lived for generations deserves further investigation by medical experts. Certainly their self-enforced isolation from the other sections of the community led to their inbreeding. Inevitably, malnutrition and unsanitary living conditions rendered them especially susceptible to deficiency and infectious diseases. There was also the climate, particularly the effect on a white skin of prolonged exposure to the sun. Such information as is available, indeed, suggests a very high susceptibility to various types of diseases compared with the rest of the white population, and, in at least one instance, with the black population.

The large scale cholera epidemic of 1854, for example, resulting in some eighteen thousand deaths, was reported to have affected very few whites, except those of the poorest class.[38] An investigation into the incidence of ankylostomiasis (hookworm), carried out in 1916 by a research team sponsored by the Rockefeller Foundation, produced results which were certainly revealing. By reason of the type of soil, hookworm was particularly prevalent in St. Andrew, St. John and St. Joseph—the parishes with the largest concentration of poor whites—and it was found to have affected 65 percent of the white people examined. These persons "showed signs of marked anaemia of the skin, lips, tongue and conjunctivae. Shortness of breath, palpitation of the heart, giddiness, pain in the pit of the stomach, pot-belly and dwarfism were common symptoms. It may be truly stated that this class of the population is sorely affected by the ravages of the hookworm disease." The incidence of the disease among blacks, however, was approximately half what it was among whites, and in any case, even when present, it apparently caused less physical deterioration than in the case of whites.[39]

Given the health factor, and the effect it must have had on the capacity of the poor whites for sustained physical work, there is little need to speculate on the less easily determinable effects of either inbreeding or the climate. These were factors which would have been likely to have had further damaging effects.

An additional factor affecting both the physical and the psychological state of the poor whites was their addiction to alcohol, though opinions vary as to the extent and seriousness of this condition. Joshua Steele had suggested that the poor whites would have been better able to withstand the effects of the climate, and to work as their forebears had done, if only they had been of temperate habits, and this point was repeated by Dr. Davy in a discourse he delivered in 1846 to the General Agricultural Society of Barbados.

> Were white labourers temperate, I have little doubt they would be able to bear the climate of the West Indies infinitely better than they have hitherto done, and that they would have a greatly better chance of escaping most of the fatal diseases peculiar to the climate; and, what is worse than bodily disease, that degeneration to which they are subject from the influence of intemperate habits and of climate combined—a degeneration of which there are too many and melancholy instances in this land, in the descendants of the original white colonists belonging to the class of labourers.[40]

Some corroboration of their predilection for alcohol was graphically provided a few years later in a letter to the press which advised that "their present state, condition, and use ... may be briefly summed up in the statement that they act as so many sponges to soak up our rum, and by a curious process of melting down of thews and sinews (to say nothing of moral qualities) to augment the nett proceeds of our distilleries." This view, not surprisingly, was questioned by another correspondent, who thought that such was no longer the position, and that few drunkards were to be found except possibly among some of the fishermen.[41] The view, however, that intemperance was among the causes of pauperism among poor whites was held very firmly by at least one member of the Poor Relief Commission—he recorded a minority opinion to this effect in the final report.

Physical deterioration was manifestly not the only reason for the inability of the poor whites to come to terms with the economic and social situation in which they found themselves. Certainly as important was their moral and possibly intellectual degeneration. In contrast, they were simultaneously persons of extreme arrogance. There was no question but that the poor whites regarding themselves as innately superior to blacks of the labouring class, and consequently considered all work of a labouring or domestic nature as beneath their station, despite the fact that they were incapable of doing other kinds of work. With Emancipation, this tendency inevitably increased. Previously they had at least had the illusion of superiority over the majority of the slaves as a result of their position as free men; some of them had had the additional special status on the plantation of military tenants. Now, however, finding themselves inexorably face to face with a large, free-black population, and with their privileged position gone, no shreds whatever of any social status were left to them. Thus, they had nothing to fall back on except the supposed superiority of their white skins.

The Poor Relief Commission Report of 1878 left no room for doubt about the realities of the position of the poor whites. They were referred to as being "manifestly a deteriorating race; miserably poor and correspondingly proud, without self-respect, idle and averse to any kind of work except fishing and the tillage of the few roods of arid sterile land which they rent . . . . In the last fifteen years there has been a marked deterioration." Attempts to help them with various kinds of poor relief had in fact, according to the report, only tended to encourage pauperism. Nor was there any doubt about their inferiority in relation to the black labouring class. A memorial from the Barbados House of Assembly, a body not normally renowned for its enlightened views, replying to a speech made in 1876 by the Earl of Carnarvon, Secretary of State for the Colonies, in which he alleged that the condition of the peasantry in Barbados was unsatisfactory, pointed out that "superficial enquirers ... are apt to confound the 40,000 agricultural labourers of the population, who are a thriving and prosperous class, with ... people of a different class, who despise agriculture, and have no definite means of subsistence; who in most cases will not work, and will not emigrate."[42]

But even as this memorial was being composed, forces were already at work, particularly in the areas of poor relief, education and emigration, which were destined to change the material situation of the poor whites over the next half century.

Chapter 7
The Era of Reform

Despite the seriousness of the situation of the poor whites in the years immediately following Emancipation, there was evidently little inclination at the time to consider any fundamental remedial measures. Just as Joshua Steele's proposals in the 1780s and J. W. Orderson's constructive criticisms of 1827 fell on deaf ears, so too, did the suggestions made by Governor Reid during the prolonged drought of 1847, while the initiative taken by Governor Hincks in 1859 in connection with emigration had to wait several years before any results were forthcoming.

It was in July 1847 that Governor Reid, after taking note of the scarcity of food, the complaints of poverty among the poor whites, and the fact that an island importing nearly all its food had no ships of its own, recommended to the Assembly that legislation be enacted to bind youngsters of the poor white class as ships' apprentices. Five months later he again drew attention in his speech at the opening of the new session of the Assembly to his proposal, emphasizing the importance of encouraging native seamen and the contribution this might make in improving the situation of the poor whites generally: "there is a large class of persons here of European descent, better fitted for navigation than for Tropical Agriculture, and it would be for the particular benefit of individuals of this class, as well as for the general interests, that they should thus occupy themselves." In the reply to the Governor's address, however, there was no reaction to his suggestion.[1] Reid had also during the same period called on "Magistrates and other influential inhabitants to stimulate the industrious cultivation of ground provisions, and promote a more general systematic attention to the Fisheries."[2]

Reid's first suggestion might well have made some contribution, albeit a small one, towards the solution not only of the unemployment problem but also the more basic one of work attitudes. The second proposal, if organised on a large enough scale, might have done much for the poor whites engaged in agriculture and fishing. Both his proposals would have helped, moreover, towards the solution of the wider problems of dependence on foreign

79

shipping and food imports. No action, however, was taken. On the other hand, Governor Hincks' later proposals for the resettlement of the poor whites, although received at the time with a marked lack of enthusiasm on the part of the Barbadian and other authorities in the area, were in fact to bear fruit at a later date. Nevertheless, for the greater part of the century, measures in connection with the poor whites remained, as they had been in the past, essentially short-term ones designed only to meet some of the most immediate problems of poverty, ill health and limited educational facilities.

It was not until the 1870s that reforms got under way that had any considerable effect on the poor white minority. During those years the previous rather half-hearted attempts to improve the systems of poor relief and education underwent a significant transformation. Commissions investigated these spheres of activity in detail and made recommendations which were to have very far-reaching effects. The new provisions for education, in particular, with their removal of the prevailing colour distinctions, were to play a very important part not only in improving the educational level of the poor whites, and hence their capacity to compete with blacks, but also in encouraging the acceptance of the principle of racial equality.

It is interesting to speculate whether the brief reign of John Pope-Hennessy as Governor of the Windward Islands from November 1875 to December 1876 had any influence on these events. His known championship of the underdog and his insistence on the urgent need for reforms might well have influenced the Barbados Legislature in this direction. In the circumstances, however, his activities had so infuriated the white hierarchy that the Secretary of State for the Colonies, Lord Carnarvon, deemed it necessary to remove him prematurely since it would have been futile to attempt any considerable reform as long as he remained Governor.[3] In fact, however, even before his arrival in Barbados, the Poor Relief Commission had been set up, the Education Commission had reported its findings, and the innovations in the emigration laws put into operation. Indeed, the sequence of events leading up to these reforms suggests that the need for them was so well established and so clearly recognised that not even a group as conservative as the Barbadian planters, rendered all the more hidebound as a reaction against the hated Pope-Hennessy, could stand in the way of their implementation.

Poor Relief

Responsibility for the poor of the island had from at least the middle of the seventeenth century rested with the local, that is, the parochial authorities, which functioned through the vestries. These consisted of a number of local persons of some standing in the community and operated more or less efficiently and equitably, according to the personalities of those who composed them. Perusal of such Vestry Minute Books as are available indicates a variety of approaches to the problems facing the vestries, though the underlying pattern remained very much the same until the changes brought about by the Poor Relief Act of 1880.

The regular method of providing aid for poor persons was by placing them on the list of "pensioners" and allotting them small sums payable monthly. Accommodation was also occasionally available, on a very limited basis, either on parish land or, as the century wore on, in almshouses of a rather primitive kind. Free medical attention was provided by appointing a local doctor as "Medical Attendant on the Poor" at a rate fixed according to the number of pensioners, including children, in the parish; and there was usually a dispensary for the provision of free medicines. Schooling of a sort was also arranged by the vestries.

This assistance to the poor had originally extended only to the white population, as the planters were responsible for the welfare of their slaves. The rise of the free coloured population, which by Emancipation was estimated to have been about half that of the total poor white population,[4] evidently made little difference to the situation. Their diligence and sense of responsibility were in sharp contrast with the attitudes of the poor whites. The Archdeacon of Barbados, in a sermon preached in 1833, commented that "a large white population are in the lowest stage of poverty and wretchedness. In the application for casual charity the number of white persons soliciting relief is far greater than that of the free coloured. The free black and coloured inhabitants have always contributed in their full proportion to the parochial taxes, for the support of the poor whites, while their own poor receive no parochial relief, but are supported by private contributions among the more wealthy of their own colour."[5]

After Emancipation, however, in spite of the fact that the black labouring population supplied most of its wants by agricultural work, there were some who needed relief. It took some little time, however, for the principle to be generally accepted that relief should be available to all. The doctor attending the poor in the parish of St. George, for example, noted that coloured persons came onto the pension list only in 1863; but by 1870 to 1874 the recipients of poor relief in every parish included persons of all colours,[6] and by 1879 the inmates of the almshouse in St. James, described as belonging to the class of the "labouring population," were evidently all black.[7] Thus, as the years went by an additional strain was thrown onto the already inadequate vestry system.

The poor relief supplied by the vestries was to some extent supplemented by other means which were usually the result of the initiative of private individuals and organisations. The Ladies' Association for the Relief of the Indigent Poor and Infirm had been the first in this field when they started their Asylum and Daily Meal Dispensary in Bridgetown in 1825. Inevitably, they ran into difficulties arising from the attitude of the planter class towards the poor whites. In 1838, a suggestion that certain premises might be available caused some elements in the Assembly to object on the grounds that the establishment of an asylum in that particular place would not be acceptable to the respectable families in the neighbourhood. Others contested this, claiming that "there was a very high enclosure, and the present establishment of the Ladies was conducted with the greatest cleanliness, order, quiet and decorum ... there could scarcely any annoyance proceed from a few quiet, aged, and infirm women, who would be too much occupied with the silent contemplation of their sorrows and reverses to disturb the neighbourhood."[8]

The organisation, however, continued to function and, following its example, other organisations providing relief in kind were started. A St. Michael's Clothing Club was in existence by 1838, and by 1877 there were seventeen such organisations throughout the island.[9] Daily Meal Societies were founded in St. Paul's district in 1840, and were operating in St. Stephen's by 1857 and in St. Matthias by 1875.[10] These were not, of course, exclusively for poor whites, though they must have benefited considerably from them. Another initiative of very considerable significance for the health of the poor was the opening of the Barbados General Hospital, supported by voluntary contributions, in 1844.[11]

There were also at this time at least two organisations for the relief of the "new" poor whites—thus providing further confirmation of the downward mobility affecting some whites previously well off and helping to swell the ranks of the existing poor whites. In about 1859 an Association for the Relief of Decayed Planters and their Destitute Families was formed in St. Lucy.[12] In 1877 there was in existence a Kindly Poor Relief Association which apparently supported thirty-eight gentlewomen "who, having seen better days, had through causes beyond their control, fallen into distressing poverty, or painfully straitened circumstances."[13]

Other private initiatives providing assistance to a limited number of poor whites took the form of bequests, usually of land, to be used for the benefit of various categories of people. In St. John, in a will of 1838, Isaac M. Massiah left six pounds per annum to "six poor widows of the white class," and Joseph Lyder, in 1843, left his property to be divided "betwixt all such whites as are bedridden, blind or so laim they cannot earn their daily bread."[14] In St. Philip, in 1848, Edward Blades left his property to be sold and the interest to be divided every year among "twelve deserving poor and respectable persons of the white population."[15] In the same parish, in 1864, Rebecca Garnes separated the beneficiaries under her will into three categories: "twelve poor creditable widows of the white population ... twelve more poor objects of the white population ... twelve more poor objects without any restrictions as to colour or complexion."[16]

Towards the end of the century attempts were made to rationalise some of the bequests by legislative action. Inevitably, as a result of the *de jure* change in the relationship between blacks and whites implied by Emancipation, as well as the glimmerings in some quarters of a more liberal attitude towards colour generally, the matter of the restriction of the post-Emancipation bequests to a particular section of the population came into question. The vestry of St. John, for example, in petitioning the Assembly in 1896 concerning the will of Joseph Lyder, stated that "in the present circumstances of the Island it is expedient that the rents and profits of the said landed property instead of being applied exclusively for the benefit of one class of poor persons ... should be applied for the purposes of poor relief generally in the said parish."[17] But although the bill as it was originally drafted had complied with the wishes of the vestry by stating that the proceeds of the property should be used "for the relief of poor persons," the Attorney General, the Hon. W. H. Greaves, pointed out during the second reading of the bill that, in view of objections to this change on the part of those who wanted the testator's wishes adhered to, the relevant words had afterward been amended and now read "to be applied by the Vestry according to the trusts contained in the will of the testator." According to the official report, this statement was greeted with cheers.[18]

The Government during this period was concerned somewhat ineffectually with attempting improvements in the existing system. It had endeavored in 1836 to protect the vestries against exploitation by passing an "Act to fix and confer settlement of rights of Paupers to dwell immoveably in some one particular Parish of this Island, and to prevent their being burthensome to Parishes they do not belong to, and to place them more effectually under the control and government of the Vestry, Churchwarden, and Justices of some particular parish." It also tried to suppress vagrancy in 1838 by instituting a system of punishments of "vagrants, Rogues and Vagabonds, and incorrigible Rogues and Vagabonds," but the act was disallowed—only to be reenacted in 1840 in rather more comprehensive terms.[19] Its main contribution, however, was the prompting of various investigations into the existing system and, eventually, the introduction of reforms.

Typically, this process was started by a suggestion from the Governor in 1850 that the administration of poor relief might be improved by the establishment of a Poor Law Board. A committee was set up to investigate returns of those receiving poor relief requested from churchwardens, and a report produced. The finding, however, was that, although the English Poor Law system was effective in that it "affords relief to the destitute, without encouraging the idle," the inauguration of a similar system was not needed in Barbados, since there was enough work for all and the great mass of people who lived by agriculture could supply their wants by working for an average of four days a week. It reasoned that, although there was, indeed, a class of indigent and helpless people who needed aid, the existing vestry system was adequate to cope with the problem.[20]

In 1869 a joint committee of Council and Assembly reported again on the general relief of the poor of the island. It divided those who needed help into two categories, those requiring permanent support and those needing temporary aid to enable them to return to work. The latter category was considered to merit assistance most, and to this end daily meal and clothing societies were recommended, along with other short-term suggestions.[21] But once again, the Assembly had failed both to produce a comprehensive report on the working of the existing system and to make any long-term recommendations for its improvement.

Then, in July 1875, when the condition of the poor of the island, according to the Administrator, had reached a point at which it was not only expedient but necessary for a full enquiry to be made into the subject, a commission was appointed.[22] After more than two years of collecting and sifting evidence, sometimes in the face of considerable difficulties, including opposition on the part of the planters and the uneasy situation attending the riots of 1876, the commission reported in November 1877.

The report and its recommendations (with appendices which were not published until 1879) were extremely wide ranging. It is worth summarizing these findings briefly, together with the suggestions made for improving the position of the class of poor whites. The commission considered, first, the situation of "poor gentlefolk" who had fallen into utter indigence, and decided that they could only be dealt with by voluntary efforts such as were already in train. The general condition of the poor whites was described as a deplorable one. It judged that the efforts at assisting them by the vestries and through various endowments which frequently gave them preferential treatment over black and coloured paupers, had for the most part been of a pauperizing character and had failed to arrest their steady descent into destitution and degradation. There had been a marked deterioration in the last fifteen years, brought about largely by their assumed attitude of superiority, which prevented them from working with coloured persons or as domestic servants; and in addition to being given to intoxicating liquor, they were incorrigible mendicants and were generally disinclined to emigrate. The example of a group which had left Barbados and settled quite satisfactorily in St. Vincent, however, suggested that some form of assisted emigration might provide at least a partial solution.

The main thrust of the commission's final recommendations concerned the reform of the existing poor relief system by the setting up of a central Poor Law Board (as had been suggested at least fifteen years earlier by Governor Colebrooke) by which to coordinate the work of local Boards of Guardians of the Poor elected by the vestries. It also recommended the reorganisation of the medical services, the expansion of the almshouse network, and the substitution of relief in kind for pensions in money.

The report and its recommendations had been presented in November 1877, but they were not debated until November 1879. The main problem of any new legislation was to find some formula that would enable relief to be available when genuinely necessary but which would not encourage habits of idleness, as had been the case under the old system. As the Governor said in his address to the Council and Assembly in February 1880, referring to the forthcoming debate on the bill: "While there should be no encouragement given to indolence or improvidence, it is equally our duty to provide for the maintenance and care of those whose infirmities prevent them from earning a livelihood, and to bring medical aid within reach of those who require it."[23]

The bill was passed on 11 May 1880. It provided for a Central Poor Law Board with a paid secretary and Poor Law Inspector, and for local Boards of Guardians of the Poor remunerated out of vestry funds. The latter were subject to specific stipulations as to the frequency of meetings and the submission of returns and estimates. It also laid down requirements for the appointment of medical officers and the establishment of dispensaries.[24] The minority view, however, expressed by the Bishop of Barbados, was that poor relief could never work efficiently on the basis of the vestries. But in spite of this, poor relief was to be transformed from an extremely amateur and haphazard system, operating virtually without any control by supervision, to a more centralised, and to some extent professional, type of organisation which at least could be expected to administer poor relief rather more efficiently and equitably than in the past, even if it might not have been able to change attitudes in those it sought to help.

Finally, in spite of the fact that the Act contained no measures relating specifically to poor whites, the proportion of poor whites receiving relief was high in comparison with poor blacks; thus any improvement in the system could be expected to have a sizable impact on them.

Education

Although the middle decades of the nineteenth century saw the beginning of the establishment of a system of primary education available to all sections of the population, this had little effect on the poor whites generally until they were brought into that system by the Education Act of 1878. Until that date most educational establishments, with a few exceptions, functioned on a segregated basis. Poor white children received their education mainly in parochial schools while black children received theirs in the primary schools, which were gradually coming into existence, as a result of the Imperial Parliament's Negro Education Grant of 1835 to 1845. The parochial schools were financed by funds available to the vestries from local taxation, supplemented in some cases by endowments, which usually also provided some measure of maintenance for the children. Of the four other schools available at that time for poor whites, three were supported by endowments, with the Central Schools in Bridgetown receiving an annual allotment from the Treasury.

The parochial schools, of which it has been noted that there were six in

1825, increased in number during the next few years until in 1838 some 250 poor-white children were receiving a somewhat rudimentary education in seven segregated schools, plus an unspecified number in schools in St. James and St. Thomas open to all classes.[25] Some indication of the level of the education was given in a report of 1857 by the School Committee to the vestry of St. George. It was noted that the twelve boys being schooled, clothed and maintained at the expense of the parish were receiving a "very simple elementary English education; which hardly advances them beyond the first rudiments of Reading, Writing and Arithmetic; and scarcely adapts them to fill any useful situation in life after the very early age at which they leave school." Since the master was resigning, it was recommended that the opportunity should be taken "to obtain the services of a man of good acquirements and responsibility; and the improved mode of teaching, tone of manners, and competition in learning which it will tend to incite in the Parish boys may redound to their advantage in every way and help to raise them from the lamentable state of ignorance and degradation into which the poor class of white people in this country have more or less fallen." The subjects to be studied were to be extended to include, in addition to the three Rs, grammar, geography, history, elements of algebra, agricultural chemistry and geometry. The twelve girls being educated by the parish received rather less attention, apart from the somewhat coy suggestion that a Ladies' Committee should be formed to assist the School Committee since "from feelings of delicacy the wants and requirements of a Girls' School can never be fully made known to a committee of gentlemen."[26] The pattern in the St. George schools of providing some degree of maintenance, which at times included boarding facilities, was repeated with variations in other parochial schools.

Of the other schools, two, the Foundation School in Christ Church and the Seminary in St. Andrew, were partially supported by their respective vestries and had between thirty and forty children.[27] Harrison's Free School was by this time mainly patronised by fee-paying pupils but still provided places for twenty-five Foundation scholars.[28] The Central Schools had been operating since 1819 for the benefit of poor white children from the entire island. During the 1830s they had an average of just over a hundred boys and rather less than a hundred girls, of whom approximately half, of both sexes, were boarders.[29] They evidently provided an adequate education by contemporary standards. A visitor to the island who was present at the annual examination of the children in 1830 found their work good, and in no sense inferior to that of the black and coloured children in a school he had visited some months earlier. He noted, however, that the physical appearance of the former, who were "very pale, delicate and plain," contrasted most unfavourably with the latter, particularly as regards "animation and power."[30] In contrast to this, Dr. Rolph, who has previously been observed to have held views diametrically opposed to those of other visitors of the same period, commented after a brief visit to what must have been the Central Schools, in 1833, that not only were their arrangements admirable but that the children had a "decent, healthy, and cheerful appearance, respectful demeanour, and becoming deportment."[31] Another commentator, in 1838, referred to these schools as "eminently efficient" in contrast to the parochial schools.[32]

The number of children being educated in these schools, ranging from the Central Schools and Harrison's Free School down to the most inadequate parochial school, cannot at this time have been more than about 550. With the total poor white population estimated very approximately at 10,000, there must have been a large number of children of school age who were either receiving no education at all, due in some cases to their living some distance from the parochial school, or who were attending "private" schools of the most primitive kind. Dr. Davy did not neglect this aspect of the poor white scene during his stay in Barbados, for he noted: "in the wilder parts of the country here and there, a school is found, chiefly for poor children of their own class, kept in aid of subsistence by a white man or woman. When by the former it is for boys, and reading and writing, and the first rules of arithmetic are taught; when by the latter, for girls, and the teaching is limited to reading and plain needlework ... and the children in reading are more exercised in the pronouncing of words, parrot-like, than in the understanding of them."[33]

Thus, the general standard of education of the poor whites can be considered abysmally low, and since it was, for the most part, segregated education, their integration into the wider community was certainly retarded. Certain developments, however, during the middle years of the century, were significant. An Education Act of 1850 provided for the giving of grants to schools for the middle classes,[34] by which was meant, generally, white people of the type who provided the managers and other middle-level plantation personnel or who farmed small plots of land on their own account. The result was that by 1869 Harrison's School, the Seminary in St. Andrew, and Christ Church Middle School were designated middle schools.[35] It may also have provided some impetus for the establishment of two private schools, the Hutchinson School in St. Philip and the Daily Meal School in Bridgetown. The former had a somewhat checkered career until it closed in 1949 due to the absence of any more poor whites to profit from it, while the latter still functions today as the Haynes Memorial School.[36] In 1849 the Central Schools abandoned their policy of discrimination and announced that in the future children were to be admitted "without distinction of race or complexion."[37] This was followed by a similar decision by the vestry of St. George but accompanied by the proviso that any coloured children should be "the children of married parents, or of parents, who, although unmarried, shall not at that time be leading an immoral life"—a decision that does not, however, seem to have been implemented.[38] By 1867 a report on the Seminary in St. Andrew by the Inspector of Schools noted that it had only white boys, but commented that this was accidental as there had been coloured boys at the school in the past and the only criterion for non-Foundationers was the ability to pay the fees.[39]

This period was one of near stagnation in the educational system of the poor whites. It was also a period in which the development of an adequate system of primary schools for the children of the newly emancipated slaves proceeded very slowly. The funds assigned under the Negro Education Grant were intended to be used for capital expenditure only. At the same time, the resources of the various missionary societies were limited, and the legislature was slow to enact the allocation of money for operational costs. Indeed, by 1844 it appears that only a very small proportion of black children were receiving any kind of formal education. Nevertheless, with the final withdrawal of the British Government's grant in 1854 and the passing of the responsibility for education entirely into the hands of the colonial legislature, the need for a more concerted approach to the whole matter of education began, albeit gradually, to be accepted.[40]

When the committee set up by the Assembly to discuss the matter reported in April 1846, there were forty-eight "national and infant" schools established under the auspices of the Bishop.[41] A grant of seven-hundred and fifty pounds a year was voted to keep these going and was continued until 1850. In that year a joint committee of the Council and Assembly made important recommendations that were to form the basis of the system by which the poor whites, nearly thirty years later, were assimilated into the general educational pattern of the island. The "Act to provide for a more extensive and general Education of the People of this Island," which resulted from these deliberations, provided for the setting up of an Education Committee, the appointment of an Inspector of Schools and a Secretary to the Committee, and the allocation of three-thousand pounds over a period of two years. Allotments from this grant were to be available to all public schools with over fifty children directly connected with any Christian church and providing religious instruction, to dame and infant schools in country districts, and to any schools set up for the education of the middle classes.[42]

The next joint committee on education, which reported in 1857, had the advantage of the advice of the Rev. Richard Rawle, principal of Codrington College, described as the "Schoolmaster-general of the Island."[43] In addition to recommending improvements in the existing system, the committee suggested a number of important innovations, such as the establishment of entirely free infant schools on a large scale, the initiation of a pupil-teacher system and of professional training for teachers, and the formation of lay education committees. Most of these recommendations were incorporated into the final Act which was passed at the end of 1858. One important additional item was the expansion of the curriculum to include, in addition to scripture, not only reading, writing and arithmetic, but also the elements of grammar, geography, history and music; the sum voted was increased to five-thousand pounds over two years.[44] By 1860 the Inspector of Schools noted an enormous improvement in the facilities available and in the number and level of teachers; the total number of schools, both primary and infant, was eighty-nine.[45]

During these forty years after Emancipation, however, no attempt had been made to look at the educational system as a whole until the commission set up in February 1874 at the instigation of, and under the chairmanship of, the Bishop of Barbados, John Mitchinson, "to fully enquire into and consider the subject of Education in this Island."[46] The Mitchinson Commission first reported in April 1875 after fourteen months of meetings, and it made detailed recommendations affecting all the several levels of education and concerning the administrative structure of the educational system. While these recommendations did not advocate any radical changes in the educational system generally, they were nevertheless of considerable importance in establishing a firm basis for the future development of that system, and particularly in improving the educational situation of the poor white population.[47]

The second part of the report, which was issued on 5 June 1875, contained the evidence on which its recommendations had been based. Among other things, it drew attention to the continuing existence in some parishes of vestry schools exclusively for white children; it commented that "the Education Committee most properly refuses to aid any school thus complexionally restricted," and it "lamented that large sums of money should be raised by taxation by the vestries of these parishes, and wasted, or nearly so, in an attempt to combine poor relief and education, with the most unsatisfactory results." It noted that there was no reason whatever for the "perpetuation of a distinction which . . . has happily become quite artificial" particularly since the children seemed to mix "on terms of social equality with their black and coloured compeers out of school." It also pointed out that many of these children would not attend school at all without the bribes of a daily meal and periodic distribution of clothing.

In connection with the education of the middle classes the commission reported that little, if anything, was being done by the State for this section of the population. There were in existence at that time only the seminary in St. Andrew and a foundation school in St. Lucy run in conjunction with a parochial white boys' school. The need, however, was to some extent being met by private schools such as the Pilgrim Place School in Christ Church (this was the middle school), and with the tuition provided in many cases by the clergy. Based on these findings, the commission recommended the abolition of colour distinctions in schools and the cessation of doles; it also made proposals for the expansion of the system of middle schools by converting certain existing endowed schools into second-grade schools.[48]

Although legislative action was not to be taken for another two years, a set of resolutions incorporating most of the commission's recommendations was adopted by the following November. Of particular interest in the context of the poor whites, and also of the principle of universal state education for children of all colours, was the sixth resolution which stated that "public money—Parochial or otherwise—shall not be granted in any circumstances, or in any form, in aid of the funds of any school endowed for the education of children of any particular complexion." The ninth resolution was also of significance in that it attempted, albeit very tentatively, to open the way to some kind of government action in connection with endowed schools by stating that "it is expedient that all the Educational Endowments in this Island, except those of Codrington College and Harrison's College, should it be practicable, be utilised for second grade education."[49] Both these items produced very interesting repercussions in the Council and the Assembly as well as in the press.

As far as the parochial schools were concerned, the Council was evidently prepared to take a far stronger line than the Assembly. It went so far as to introduce an "Act to abolish Parochial Schools now restricted to white children exclusively." This Act referred in its preamble to the parochial schools "supported in some cases entirely, and in others in the greater part out of taxation levied on all classes in the Parishes in question by the Vestry, and from which schools the children of black and coloured persons are excluded," and it went on to state that "whereas such a restriction is opposed to the principle of the Act passed by the Imperial Parliament for the emancipation of the black and coloured classes and that part from parochial or other funds levied on all classes are declared to be unlawful." The teachers and others concerned in them were to be liable to a fine or imprisonment.[50] The Act was passed by the Council on 19 September 1876, but at its first reading in the Assembly a week later, Conrad Reeves, then a member of the Assembly and later, as Chief Justice, to be the first black man in the British Empire to receive a knighthood,[51] indicated that he considered that a mountain was being made out of a molehill. He pointed out that the report of the commission "dealt with other things besides this colour prejudice, which was one of the fossil remains of a byegone age," and that not only was the amount appropriated to the white schools very small but that, in any case, they were only nominally for white boys.[52] The bill was not proceeded with in the Assembly, presumably because the matter was regarded as having been adequately covered in the sixth resolution resulting from the commission's recommendations. The President of the Council regretted, however, that so important a measure introduced in the Council had not been proceeded with in the Assembly.[53]

The question of the endowed, or partially endowed, school was raised in the Assembly in debate on the resolutions. The schools concerned were Foundation in Christ Church, Hutchinson's in St. Philip, and the Seminary in St. Andrew. There was evidently a difference of opinion as to whether the money available to those schools should be appropriated for second-grade schools open to all, or whether they should continue to be run according to the wishes of the testator. The matter was concluded by a decision that the resolution concerning schools restricted to white children referred only to those receiving public money, and therefore the endowed schools could continue as before.[54]

This provoked a debate in the columns of the *West Indian* concerning the Hutchinson School but which had some relevance to the whole question of these bequests. The editor had referred to the difficulty, in connection with this particular school, of carrying out the testator's stipulations "for the public advantage." A trustee of the school retorted that Mr. Hutchinson had had good sense: "He lived among a large number of the lower middle class of whites who could not be induced to send their children to the ordinary Primary School, and so, making allowance for the 'hardness of their hearts' he established a school for their special behest." This was extremely important for the "class from which we draw that all-important body in the community, our 'Estate-assistants.'" The editor concurred in supporting the principle of bequests being earmarked for particular purposes, including aid for specific classes. He outlined the sad history of the poor whites and he concluded: "As a class they are fast disappearing. The time for them is gone by, and they must go too. Perhaps the school in St. Philip will help them to rise in the world, by giving them a better education."[55] In fact, legislative provision was made in 1887 for the expansion of the school but, almost immediately afterwards, the funds apparently disappeared, and, for a time at least, the school was closed.[56]

Although the principle of abolishing colour restrictions in education, and thus the closing of the parochial schools, had already been accepted, the uselessness of these schools for educational purposes in addition to their undesirability for social reasons was confirmed in the report on education, which was presented in February 1877 by John A. Savage, Inspector of Schools for Jamaica, who had been sent to Barbados by the Colonial Office. He was required to examine in detail the work of the elementary schools, as he himself took pains to point out, in order to supplement the work of the earlier Mitchinson Commission. After describing in his report the nature of the parochial schools, and the commission's findings, Savage remarked:

> These parochial schools are really not needed. In the parish of St. Joseph I found one of them located in a district between two Primary Schools that are under Government inspection, one about a mile and the other two or three miles off. In one of these 25 and in the other 40 white children were found mixed with a large number of coloured children, and in every respect treated alike. In this respect the two primaries are far superior to the Parochial Schools—the instruction in the latter being on the whole mechanical and devoid of practical intelligence, and its existence here tends not only to keep up an injurious class prejudice but also to prevent its pupils from availing them-

selves of the better instruction in the schools under Government inspection.[57]

After the very comprehensive report of the Mitchinson Education Commission, Savage's report, and the extensive public debate on the whole
matter, it remained only for the appropriate legislation to be enacted. The bill
had its first reading in March 1878 and was eventually passed on 9 December
1878. It embodied most of the recommendations of the Mitchinson Commission and the subsequent resolutions including the ban on the use of public
money for schools maintaining colour restrictions and on the distribution of
bribes to induce children to attend school. It shelved the controversial matter
of turning the endowed schools into second grade schools by providing for
the Central Schools to become second grade schools for boys and girls
respectively; for Lodge School to make second grade education available for
boys from St. Philip, St. John and St. Joseph; and for schemes for additional
second-grade schools to be laid before the legislature.[58]

The implementation of the Act proceeded with reasonable speed. Of the
four parochial schools still in existence at the time, those in St. Andrew and
St. Joseph closed at once, while those in St. George and St. Lucy, which were
still operating on a segregated basis but without official aid, succumbed by
1882 and became ordinary primary schools.[59] By 1879 the Central School for
boys had begun to be turned into a second grade school later to become
Combermere School.[60] The Central School for girls turned into the second
grade Queen's College, which was raised to the status of a first grade school
in 1884 as had been provided for in the 1878 Act.[61] The three existing middle
schools, although not referred to specifically in the Act, had by the early 1880s
conformed with its spirit. The Seminary in St. Andrew became the
second-grade Alleyne School,[62] Christ Church Middle School came under the
control of the Education Board,[63] and St. Lucy's Middle School became the
Parry School.[64] Only Hutchinson's School in St. Philip and the Daily Meal
School in Bridgetown remained as endowed schools restricted to poor whites.

Although no reference had been made in the Act to existing educational
trusts other than those specifically concerned with operating schools, the
suitability in the future of continuing to utilise them along the same restricted
lines as before was called sharply into question during this period, as has
already been seen in the case of trusts devoted to poor relief. The problem
was again that of wills dating back to the period of slavery that referred only
to "poor people," while obviously meaning poor white people. The solution
which was found was to interpret the bequests literally. Thus in the case of
post-Emancipation wills referring specifically to poor whites, the restriction
was maintained, as has been noted in the case of Hutchinson's School. In the
case of pre-Emancipation wills, where there had been no need for any
reference to colour, the funds were in future used for the poor generally.

The Bulkeley and Butcher bequests, both in the parish of St. George and still in operation at the present day, came under review in 1892 when the Solicitor General asked for details of funds devoted by private persons to charitable and education purposes.[65] The former, which dated back to 1688, had passed through many vicissitudes over the years. During the nineteenth century it had been used to help finance the parochial schools but this had ceased after the new Education Act came into force. The vestry wanted to use the money to pay fees for poor children at elementary schools and also to provide a small number of exhibitions at first or second grade schools. After considerable debate, during which it was conceded that the vestry's intention of making these awards to "persons in straitened circumstances" was in accord with the testator's wishes, the Bulkeley Trust Fund Act of 1894 was passed, incorporating the vestry's proposals.[66]

The Butcher bequest, dating back to 1777, had been used for the education, clothing, and maintenance of six poor white boys at St. George's Parochial School. The Butcher Trust Fund Act of 1894 made certain beneficial financial proposals and increased the number of poor boys to be helped. Later, however, with the introduction of free education, the fund was no longer used for educational purposes but only for providing clothing for poor boys.[67]

As in the case of the Poor Relief Act of 1880, the reforms introduced by the Education Act of 1878 were not intended specifically to ameliorate the conditions of the poor whites in preference to the blacks. Both were intended to bring about improvements in the situation of the poorer classes generally and, therefore, were of necessity applicable to the position of poor whites. The Education Act, however, made a particularly important contribution when it provided not only for the better administration of education generally but also for the incorporation of the poor whites into the school system. The effect was to improve the educational situation of the poor whites by taking them out of the inferior parochial schools and into the still inadequate, but nevertheless superior, primary schools, and thus from a totally stagnant and moribund system into one which was at least in the process of being transformed. At the same time, their self-imposed isolation was radically breached; the enforced mixing of the children in the same schoolroom, while not extending to the broader world outside, was to bring about a recognition with the passage of time of the community of shared interests on the part of what had hitherto been two quite separate sections of the population.

Emigration

The emigration of poor whites from Barbados, a phenomenon which had existed from the first years of settlement until early in the nineteenth century, had always been regarded as a source of concern, since it decreased the number of white people available for a variety of functions, in particular, the manning of the Militia and the maintaining of some kind of numerical racial balance with the black slave population. With the radically changed situation brought about by Emancipation, however, it was to acquire quite a different significance, and, indeed, by the second half of the century to become a major factor in attempting to solve the unemployment problems of the poor whites.

The years immediately following the termination of the apprenticeship system in 1838 were marked by official attempts to curb emigration, particularly in view of the Barbados planters' wish to keep up the numbers of labourers on their plantations.[68] Legislation was enacted in 1836 to regulate the emigration of labourers, and also of skilled artificers, who were going off the island, frequently leaving their families behind them; and in 1839 legislation was passed to prevent children under sixteen from being lured away without the knowledge of their relatives.[69] In many cases the emigration figures were not large—the official figure for the period between 1836 and the first half of 1839 did not amount to more than 410, the majority of whom were thought, in any case, to have remained in Bridgetown. It was not until a British Guiana Emigration Office started operations in August 1839 that labourers began leaving Barbados on a large scale.[70] The conditions of recruitment and service were so bad, however, and returning emigrants had such horrific tales to tell, that in September 1840 an Act was passed making it an offence for anyone to induce labourers or artificers to leave the island.[71]

Unemployment figures at the same time were increasing, however, and in the next few years a fairly strong body of opinion developed which considered that the only way to solve this problem of unemployment was through emigration. Even an editorial in the *Barbadian* supporting this view could state rather hard-heartedly: "the 18,000 who died in the cholera epidemic (of 1854) were not missed."[72] By 1864 legislation had been enacted which it was hoped would "promote a healthful stream of emigration and one sufficient to relieve the island of that portion of its population unable to find employment at home," but which in fact made few changes in the existing law except to appoint a Superintendent of Emigration,[73] although no actual appointment was made until 1873. The Act itself was soon to be amended in one important respect—it had previously prohibited the appointment of emigration agents coming from any country offering to pay bounties to Barbadian emigrants; this was repealed by an Act passed in September 1873.[74] This was to mark the start of large-scale emigration which before then, in the years 1861 to 1871, had been estimated at 20,408.[75]

The poor whites would not have been much affected by these developments. They did not, generally speaking, fall into the category of "agricultural labourers," even if in fact they were earning a living by this means. They would have been no more interested in the efforts of the emigration agents to recruit labourers than the agents were in them. Nevertheless, there is evidence of a group of poor whites from Christ Church going to Demarara, some time during the earlier part of the period, and perishing in the swamps there,[76] and there were occasional poor white emigrants who left Barbados either under their own steam or as a result of recruitment. At the same time, the principle of solving the problem of unemployment through emigration clearly applied just as much to poor whites as it did to poor blacks, though the incentives might need to be different.

Governor Hincks, who was at least as concerned as his predecessor about the need to take some kind of action to attempt to solve the problem of the poor whites, embarked on his efforts to resettle them outside Barbados at the beginning of 1859 with a despatch to the Secretary of State for the Colonies in which he described the background and current situation of the poor whites, and suggested that emigration to neighbouring West Indian colonies, where they could acquire small allotments of land and earn their living by cultivating them, might prove to be their salvation. He cited St. Vincent as being particularly suitable; in fact, he had already been in unofficial communication with Eyre, the Lieutenant Governor, who had given him to understand that the plan would be practicable.[77]

During the next few months reactions to his initiative came back not only from London, where there was general approval, but also from St. Vincent, Jamaica, the Bahamas, and Grenada. In the case of St. Vincent, Eyre was no longer in office, and the proposal was turned down by the Legislature on the grounds that the immigrants would not be available for agricultural purposes and might, indeed, become a charge on the colony. Also at work might have been fears that grants of land given free to Barbadians might cause dissatisfaction among its own labouring population.[78] From Jamaica the reply came that the only lands available were too humid and cold for Barbadians, but, in any case, there were neither funds nor machinery available to help in their resettlement.[79] The Governor of the Bahamas commented at length to the Secretary of State for the Colonies that the poor whites of Barbados were very similar to the lowest rank of the Bahamian whites, and that not only was there no work which they would be capable of doing but "they would be lazy enough to corrupt by their example, the negroes whom they are foolish enough in their ignorance to despise: and that so far from ever adding to the wealth and honour of the Colony, they would become both a burden and a discredit." Immigration was required, he conceded, but of West Africans, Indians and Chinese as hired labourers.[80] Only from Grenada did an encouraging response come, to the effect that Crown land in the Grand Etang area in the center of the island would be available, and that an industrious agricultural community located there could be both prosperous and a great asset to the island.[81]

At this stage, the matter was put before the Barbados House of Assembly. The Administrator, in the Governor's absence, appeared from his covering note to the relevant documents to have stifled the Grenada suggestion by saying that "before this scheme could be effected, however, the lands would

have to be cleared at an expense, and, if the whites themselves were engaged
in the work, at a cost of life, which puts it almost out of the question." When
the Governor referred to the whole matter in his speech at the opening of the
new session in December 1859, and requested the cooperation of the
legislature, he received a somewhat lukewarm assurance from both the Assembly and Council, that they would give due consideration to any practical
proposals.[82]

In fact the goodwill of the Legislature was soon to be put to the test.
Evidently the Governor of Jamaica's rejection of the offer of the poor white
Barbadians had stirred up considerable debate in the Jamaican press,[83] and
this resulted in a Jamaican by the name of Anderson coming to Barbados in
order to arrange for the shipment to Jamaica of a small group of poor whites
on an experimental basis. The Governor invited the Assembly to vote a sum
not exceeding one-hundred pounds to defray the cost of transport, but doubt
was expressed by members as to Anderson's precise obligations and the
proposal was turned down.[84] The *Barbadian,* in an editorial on the subject,
regretted the action of the House; Anderson had been well vouched for in
letters from the Governor of Jamaica to his colleague in Barbados, and thus
the Assembly's criticism appeared to have been unfounded.[85]

In spite of these rebuffs, Governor Hincks was obviously not a person to
abandon a cause which he regarded as just. He returned again to the attack in
a despatch to the Duke of Newcastle, then Secretary of State for the Colonies,
countering allegations that the poor whites of Barbados were idle and
improvident with letters from local dignitaries testifying as to their in-
dustriousness, thrift and suitability for resettlement, and reviving the question
of emigration to St. Vincent. He considered that the objections raised in St.
Vincent were totally invalid and attributed this opposition to the local policy
of refusing to sell Crown lands to the labouring classes. He made an
impassioned plea that "the selfish views of some gentlemen on St. Vincent
should not be allowed to operate in obstructing a scheme of such benevolence" and concluded: "if Your Grace should decide that no Crown lands in
St. Vincent are to be alienated until the Government of that Country in
which the influence of the Planters predominates, shall yield their consent, all
hopes of effecting the removal of the 'Poor Whites' must be abandoned."[86]

The Colonial Land and Emigration Commissioners, commenting a little
acidly on what they clearly regarded as Governor Hincks' *volte-face* in the
matter of the physical and moral qualities of the poor whites, expressed the
view that the St. Vincent Legislature might be prepared to reconsider the
matter if it was explained again, making clear that any initial settlement
would be in the nature of a small scale experiment, and that the Barbados
Legislature would finance the whole undertaking. In the event, the Governor
was given the authority to raise the matter once again with St. Vincent, and, if
they agreed, to carry on with the project.[87] At this stage, in the absence of
evidence of any official negotiations with St. Vincent, and in light of his

disillusionment with its Government, it is likely that Hincks pursued the matter privately. In any event, his speech to the Barbados Legislature in January 1861 referred to his belief that it might be possible to launch a pilot scheme in St. Vincent and asked for a loan to make this possible: "this would have the most beneficial results to a portion of the population which has very great claim on your consideration, and which I am led to fear will ere long be unable to procure the means of subsistence unless some measures should be devised for their relief." His request, however, fell on deaf ears; the replies to his address made no reference whatsoever to it.[88]

In spite of the total lack of enthusiasm on the part of both legislatures —which was inexplicable in purely rational terms in view of Barbados' need to get rid of her surplus population and St. Vincent's to import extra labour—the Governor's initiatives were already having some results. As far as Barbados was concerned, there was at least the beginning of some interest in emigration among the poor whites; the Governor had, for example, ascertained that there were a number of families in St. John who were prepared to sell what they had and go to St. Vincent. This interest, if not enthusiasm, may also have been increased by press support for the Governor's final offensive against the Assembly. This was described by the Editor of the *Barbadian* as an attempt to "rescue from destruction a body of people who were once the mainstay of the proprietary body, but who are now sneered at as 'the everlasting poor whites.'"[89]

In St. Vincent the immigration of Barbadians was by no means a new phenomenon. During the years immediately preceding the census of 1861 there had evidently been a considerable influx of immigrants from Barbados as well as from elsewhere.[90] Some of these had been white. According to the figures quoted for the period September 1858 to February 1859, a total of 489 Barbadians recruited by a special agent for work on the estates had included about 100 white people.[91] White Barbadian immigration, which seems to have been initially inspired by a resident of St. Vincent, was not therefore without precedent; it may well, however, have been influenced, whether directly or indirectly, by Governor Hincks.

The settlement of whites on Dorsetshire Hill, a few miles northeast of Kingstown, which is identifiable to this day, was the result of this early emigration initiative. The Reverend H. W. Laborde, who had been Rector of Kingstown since 1852, told the representative of the Barbados Poor Relief Commission in 1876 that the first group of poor whites from Barbados who settled on Dorsetshire Hill came as the result of a request made by Dr. Checkley of St. Vincent to Dr. Bradshaw, the Rector of St. Joseph in Barbados. With the initial assistance of advances from the proprietors of the estate, they had leased small plots of forest land, cleared the wood, and cultivated the soil. Healthy and hard-working, they had succeeded, according to Mr. Laborde, in making quite a comfortable living, and by the mid-1870s had established for themselves on Dorsetshire Hill a flourishing settlement of some three to four-hundred people. In addition, some of the people from Barbados had gone to Bequia, an island in the Grenadines a short distance from St. Vincent, where they had been less successful and subsisted mainly by growing corn.[92] Laborde's evidence was reasonably accurate in spite of some vagueness as to the precise date of first settlement, for an official comment made in 1865 on St. Vincent's population figures referred to the inclusion of the "Barbadian white tradesmen and labourers."[93] Moreover, an analysis of the entries in the parish registers for residents of Dorsetshire Hill for the years 1860 to 1875 shows that there was a gradually increasing population of persons with names of recognisably Barbadian origin, some of whom can be traced back to the eastern parishes of Barbados.

In Laborde's day the people of Dorsetshire Hill concentrated entirely on agriculture and kept themselves very much to themselves. This pattern began changing considerably, however, by the middle decades of the twentieth century. Although there are still many tall, thin, and prematurely wrinkled white people to be seen tending their crops or engaging in other agricultural pursuits, many of them have moved away from Dorsetshire Hill and into the professions and business. Similarly in Bequia, the white Barbadian immigrants who originally settled on the Mount Pleasant estate have turned from agriculture to other occupations, such as commercial lobster fishing or serving aboard yachts and bulk carriers, in the process establishing a strong fishing and seafaring tradition which contrasts with the mainly agricultural pursuits of the Dorsetshire Hill community.[94]

A few poor whites from Barbados also went to Grenada during the 1860s. It seems likely, however, that the impetus for their settlement on Mount Moritz was provided by the shipment in 1875 of a small group of about a dozen men and women to work on a cocoa plantation.[95] This plantation was almost certainly on the Mount Moritz estate and may well have formed the nucleus for the initial poor white settlement which was to develop during the next thirty or so years. During the 1880s there were grandparents and parents of the present generation of "Mount Moritz Bajans" living on estates such as Beausejour and Grand Mal in the flat coastal and valley areas surrounding Mount Moritz, but a move to the cooler hillside estate of Mount Moritz was evidently made as and when leasehold land became available.[96] The oldest inhabitant of Mount Moritz, who was ninety-eight in 1973, had followed just this pattern. He had come to Grenada in 1887 and had lived free on the Beausejour estate before moving to Grand Mal, and then to Mount Moritz. By 1940 there were forty-three tenants, almost all evidently of Barbadian origin, living on the Mount Moritz estate of 121 acres, and cultivating plots of land, or in some cases several plots, but none of which were larger than one and one-half acres, and some of them very much smaller.[97] At this time the "Mount Moritz Bajans" were poor, hard-working market-gardeners, who walked to the market in St. George's to sell their produce, and who were either disregarded or treated with scorn by the rest of the population. There was a ditty popular in the 1930s, shouted by the children of St. George at their poor white schoolfellows, which began:

> Cricket gill and dry bonavis',
> Good enough for poor backra.

Quantitatively this community constituted over one-half of the people included in the 0.9 percent of the population enumerated as white in the Grenada census of 1946.[98] Qualitatively, it evidently had a potential for development which has become manifest during the last twenty years, during which time many of its members have moved from peasant agriculture into the professions and business. Moreover, although frequently still resident in their original area of settlement, unlike their counterparts in St. Vincent, they are rapidly becoming absorbed into the life of the community as a whole.

Governor Hincks had thus, in practical terms, been more successful than he could have realised at the time. However, in addition to having inspired the foundation of reasonably satisfactory settlements in St. Vincent and Grenada, he had also by his actions indicated the desirability of giving special consideration to encouraging the emigration of poor whites. This development was to be incorporated into the legislation concerning emigration from the 1870s onwards.

In the Emigration Act of 1873, arrangements were made for the sum of 200 pounds a year to be at the disposal of the Governor in Council to "aid persons of the class above labourers and artisans to emigrate from Barbados to neighbouring countries." Little use was made of this concession; no more than eleven applications were granted during the years 1873 to 1877, of which five were in 1877. In that year the Superintendent of Emigration referred in his annual report to the emigration of labourers as affecting the balance of the population and stated that the operation of the grants "tended in some measure to adjust the social balance." He went on to state that the funds were intended "to aid the members of the middle classes, who, in the severe competition for employment, are unable to earn a living in the island."[99] In 1881 the amount available for this purpose, defined this time as being intended "to assist persons of the poorer classes who would be likely to better their conditions by emigration," was increased to 300 pounds.[100] This may have represented a limited response to the acceptance given in the Poor Relief Report of 1877 to the principle of emigration as a means of helping to improve the situation of the poor whites.

A further attempt to grapple with the problem was made by a committee appointed by the abortive Emigration Commission set up in 1893. The committee proposed, *inter alia*, the establishment of a Central Emigration Agency through which "many of those poor whites, especially females, who are physically unable to work in the fields under the blaze of a tropical sun, might be helped to get to a colder climate," and went on to say: "we are encouraged to press this suggestion, because with scarcely a single exception the emigration of this class to Canada and the U.S., which has been carried out to a limited extent during the last few years by private enterprise, has proved a complete success."[101] Indeed, an American visitor in 1887 commented on the emigration of young white men from Barbados to the United States and asserted that "our country receives no braver, more resolute, or success-compelling recruits than these fairspoken, quick-witted Bims."[102]

The committee's recommendation came to nothing at the time but no doubt provided the inspiration for the Act of 1897 which, with unexpected originality, provided for the formation of the Victoria Emigration Society, with which to commemorate Queen Victoria's diamond jubilee. The object was to assist poor white women to emigrate. The legal draftsmen must have gone through tortures over the wording of this Act. As has been seen in the case of previous legislation, it was not acceptable to call a spade a spade, or rather, a poor white a poor white, and thus resort had to be made to a variety of circumlocutions which were inevitably open to a number of interpretations. In this case, the original idea was obviously to assist poor white women who were described in the original draft as "women in reduced circumstances." There was objection to this phrase during the passage of the bill through the Assembly on the grounds that it referred only to a particular class; the wording was therefore changed to the somewhat unwieldy phrase "poor women who are compelled to earn their living but are unable to do so in Barbados."[103] By 1900 the Society had been responsible for the emigration of 179 white and 50 coloured women.[104] No doubt it had made a useful contribution towards solving the problem of unemployed women. The slightly comic appearance presented by this whole operation is enhanced by the fact that in 1913 the United States Department of Labor was to find that this type of assisted emigration brought the immigrants within the prohibited classes and thus rendered them liable to deportation; it did not, however, intend to take action against those women who had already been admitted.[105] A stop was thus effectively put to the activities of the Victoria Emigration Society as far as the United States was concerned, though women continued to be assisted to emigrate elsewhere, usually to Canada.

No estimate of the number of poor whites who emigrated during this period, either with or without official assistance, is possible. Taking into account the emigration to St. Vincent and Grenada, the 179 women disposed of by the Victoria Emigration Society and sundry other emigrants, the number cannot have been inconsiderable. Nevertheless, the Colonial Secretary, reporting on the Blue Book for 1899, summed up the situation in fairly pessimistic terms:

> The condition of the poorer class of whites is becoming pressing. They are simply without resources; young men and women willing to work, are unable to find work; or if they do,

it is at such starvation prices that they can barely live. For this class the Government does what its means permit, and many emigrants are sent to the US and Canada each year, for the most part finding work and prosperity; but the aid given is but a drop in the bucket to what is needed.[106]

Inadequate as its results might have been at that time, a process had been set in motion which was to gain considerable momentum during the early years of the twentieth century. With the various other changes under way in the pattern of life of people generally, and the poor whites in particular, the decline in the situation of the poor whites which had commenced more than two centuries earlier would eventually be reversed.

Chapter 8
Rehabilitation of the Poor Whites

It was some time before the reforms introduced during the last quarter of the nineteenth century began to have any effect. Indeed, for at least the first three decades of the twentieth century visitors were struck by the same features of the "Redlegs" as had shocked their forerunners in the previous century. Their physical appearance had evidently not improved; one traveller to Barbados in 1909 remarked that "toil has left its mark on the 'Redlegs,' and exposure to the weather has bleached them. The stiff salt winds have inflamed their eyes in a chronic bloodshot condition; their lips are sore-looking and galled from the wind and the sun, and even their eyebrows are bleached to a ghastly whiteness; while huge freckles spot their brick-coloured faces, and their sun-dried hands and feet are marked with horn like scales."[1] These physical characteristics still seemed to be matched by their mental and moral qualities; the general impression given was one of uselessness, hopelessness, and degeneracy.

Nevertheless, there were also the beginnings of attempts to provide some explanation of, and perhaps justification for, their situation. As late as 1931 the "Redlegs" were described as ragged and degenerate looking. There was, however, at least an awareness of the fact that observers from abroad were likely to be affected by culture-shock: "such poverty-stricken members of the white race invariably excite comment in a land where one expects the lower strata of society to be composed wholly of blacks."[2] There was also more of a preparedness than in the previous century to see them as victims of their wretched condition. They might be "a joyless company of pariahs, housed in wretched huts and making a flabby pretence at living as fishermen," but "long intermarriage, long living in the tropics, long centuries of purposeless existence" had "left them utterly degenerate, anaemic in mind and body, sapless and nerveless, mere shadows of once sturdy men."[3] Their history was described by another writer as "almost incredible, and their present plight pitiable, and the worst of it is there is apparently no possibility of ameliorating their conditions."[4]

However, these same observers, depressing as they may have sounded, chanced to pinpoint certain features which were, in fact, indicative of some change for the better. The poor whites were now described as "strenuous workers" who, while not sharing their social life with blacks, nevertheless treated their black employers with the respect due to them.[5] Someone commented on seeing these "ragged barefoot men and women, tilling the fields among the black and coloured workers."[6] Most importantly, by 1908 it was possible to observe that "their number now is few."[7]

Some observers, however, were unduly pessimistic. What doubtlessly impaired their vision in describing the "Redleg" situation was the fact that they were looking for certain stereotypes, based on their previous reading of published accounts, unaware that those poor whites they now found were no longer necessarily typical. And owing to their lack of background knowledge of the local scene, they lacked the means of recognising those "Redlegs" who had made good. During these years, as will be seen, a very significant improvement had come about in the position of the poor whites generally.

The importance of emigration in achieving this change can hardly be overestimated. As a result of the reduction of the size of the white population, various other factors affecting the lives of those left behind came into play. Their reduced numbers gave them more room to maneuver with increased possibilities of seizing such opportunities of employment as came their way. Many of them received financial support in the form of remittances from those of their relatives who had found some degree of prosperity abroad; thus many were able to escape from conditions of abject poverty. In addition, those who remained found it possible, owing to their reduced numbers, to enter into closer contact with the blacks among whom they lived. Together with the change in the educational system already noted, such contact helped to remove them from the virtual isolation into which they had previously been cast.

The pattern of emigration was already well established by the end of the nineteenth century, and as late as the first decade of the twentieth century it was still regarded as of prime importance in solving the problem of the "Redlegs." An interesting initiative was taken in 1909 by George O'Donnell Walton, a Barbadian medical doctor who lived in St. Joseph but who had at one time also been "Medical Attendant on the Poor" in the parish of St. Thomas. He was not only profoundly interested in the history and circumstances of the poor whites but also prepared to take some kind of positive action to try to improve their situation. His correspondence with N. Darnell Davis, Comptroller of Customs in British Guiana and an amateur historian with a great knowledge of, and interest in, Barbados,[8] shows that he had made an appeal to the well-known American philanthropist Andrew Carnegie to finance the establishment in the Canadian northwest of a settlement for the poor whites of Barbados as well as subsidizing their passages there. This appeal was supported by an article on white slavery by Davis, and was couched in such terms as might have been expected to tug at the heartstrings of the emigre Scot.[9] However, nothing came of Dr. Walton's initiative.[10]

He did make one more effort. In a letter to the *Spectator* a few years later, Dr. Walton described the situation of "the wreckage of our race, the poor white refuse known to derision and scorn as the Redlegs of Barbados, the wreckage of England's civil wars;" he outlined their origins, the contribution they had made to the settlement of Barbados before the importation of the slaves, and the part they had played in "laying the stepping-stones of Empire through the length and breadth of the blue Caribbean." He then referred to the oblivion into which they had fallen, "hiding with honest racial pride their undeserved degeneration," and ended with an appeal for help so that the younger people at least might be assisted to emigrate, that someone might "extend a saving hand to this wastrel of an Imperial race, and so save them from poverty, degradation, and worse."[11]

The article in fact inspired the Governor of Queensland to raise with the Colonial Office in London the possibility of the emigration of the "Redlegs" to Queensland, and the Governor of Barbados was asked to report on their current situation. The replies elicited by the Governor from his enquiries on the subject, from members of the Legislative Assembly for St. Andrew and St. John, the Rector of the Parish of St. Joseph, and the Poor Law/Public Health Inspector, indicated that the situation of the "Redlegs" had so much improved in recent years, partly as a result of their emigration to Canada and the United States, that it was not such as to warrant their assisted emigration.[12] It is unfortunate that Dr. Walton's views on the verdicts of his fellow countrymen were not recorded.

In any case, Dr. Walton's initiatives were somewhat belated, and, even if they had succeeded, might not have made much difference to their situation at this stage. White people in general, and poor whites in particular, were already emigrating in fair numbers. Official comment on the decrease in the total white population of Barbados from 15,613 in 1891 to 12,063 in 1911 attributed it both to the withdrawal of British troops, and to the exodus of whites to the United States and Canada, with the latter movement continuing since opportunities for employment in the colony were very limited.[13] The decrease in the numbers of whites, in fact, continued, though at a slower pace: the total white population fell to 10,429 in 1921 and to 9,839 in 1946.[14] The figure of 9,354 provided by the 1970 census is evidently still decreasing, if there is any truth in a newspaper report of February 1974 that some 700 white persons were expected to leave Barbados for Australia and New Zealand shortly thereafter.[15] While no breakdown into separate categories of whites is available, the large number of families of "Redleg" origin who to-day can boast of a majority of their members living abroad suggests that a fair proportion of the total number of emigrants would be poor whites.

Attention has already been paid to the significance of the Education Act of 1878 in bringing poor white children out of the old segregated parochial schools and into the more efficient primary schools attended by the majority of the population. Although subsequent investigations were to draw attention to the unsatisfactory nature of the whole system of education in Barbados, at the time of the original Education Act this was irrelevant in the context of the poor whites. What was important was that they were no longer disadvantaged by comparison with blacks of the same social class. The change itself appears to have come about without any serious opposition. By 1913 the rector of St. Joseph, with its large poor white population, commented that practically the whole generation of "Redlegs" was being educated at the elementary schools of the colony and that this widespread education was having a considerable effect on their capacity to better themselves.[16]

Nevertheless, there were inevitably some poor white children who evaded the elementary schools and continued to receive some sort of inferior segregated schooling. A visitor to Barbados in 1921 suggested that there was a tendency to send the girls to private schools since it was considered "not safe" to let them attend the elementary schools.[17] Although there were a number of private secondary schools catering mainly for upper class white children, there appear to have been only two private schools that were operating specifically for poor whites which were still in existence in the twentieth century. The Hutchinson School in St. Philip, which had previously only narrowly avoided being turned into a second grade school open to all, eventually closed in 1949 as there were by that date virtually no more poor whites left in the parish.[18] The Daily Meal School in Bridgetown, renamed the Haynes Memorial School, still continues in existence as a curious anachronism, perpetuating as it does some of the most unsatisfactory features of the old system which the Act resulting from the Mitchinson report had sought to eradicate.

Another very important factor in bringing about the rehabilitation of the poor whites was the gradual improvement in poor relief, including medical aid, as well as the public health service. The latter, as was the case with poor relief, was administered by the vestries, through a system of Commissioners and a Board of Health. In 1908, however, legislation was enacted consolidating the various Acts of the island relating to public health, and in 1912 provision was made for the appointment of a combined Poor Law and Public Health Inspector, who was to be a full-time salaried official.[19]

The very first annual report on the public health of Barbados drew attention to the prevalence of ankylostomiasis, particularly in the parishes of St. Andrew, St. Joseph and St. John,[20] parishes with very high percentages of poor whites. Reference has already been made to their vulnerability to this disease, which may have been largely responsible for their physical deterioration over the years. The report produced in 1917 by a medical research team left no doubt about the urgent need for some kind of action to control the disease. A survey of the sequence of events after the presentation of the report, however, reveals not only incompetence but sheer ignorance and obstinacy on the part of the vestries, and a total lack of any responsible control by the Board of Health.

Two years after the publication of this report, the Governor, in his address to the Legislative Council and Assembly in September 1919, referred to measures to eradicate ankylostomiasis as having been under consideration but no action having been taken owing to the war. It would appear that detailed recommendations concerning action to be taken had been made early in that year, but the vestries had refused to do anything. The St. Philip vestry, for example, had commented that the expenditure of some five to ten-thousand pounds "in an attempt to minimise the incidence of a disease that gravely affects the health of only circumscribed sections of the population would not be justified."[21]

Far wider issues were at stake, however, than simply the control of hookworm, important as that indubitably was. As a result of the discussion which the Barbados Public Health Inspector had held with the Colonial Advisory Medical and Sanitary Committee, and the recommendations resulting from that meeting, the Secretary of State for the Colonies wrote in September 1923 to the Governor of Barbados frankly criticizing the unsatisfactory state of the health and sanitary conditions in the colony. He was particularly severe on the existing system by which responsibility for sanitation was left to local authorities, that is, to the vestries. He referred to the committee's regret that the antihookworm campaign had been abandoned owing to a lack of interest on the part of the parish authorities, and he drew attention to its insistence that preventative sanitary measures were of primary importance in controlling diseases such as ankylostomiasis and typhoid.[22] The Secretary of State's despatch eventually reached the press in Barbados, though initially the Board of Health would not accept responsibility for its dissemination. It apparently remained unnoticed except by the *Barbados Herald*, which launched a campaign in terms as strong as those contained in the despatch itself. A leading article noted that it was an "everlasting disgrace for Barbadians to be living under present conditions" with the highest infant mortality rate in the British Empire. Further articles by Clennell Wickham attacked the complacency of Barbadians and their total neglect of the poor.[23]

The Governor in July 1925 resubmitted the despatch of the Secretary of State to the Assembly, and he asked for its reply to a previous recommendation that he had made for the setting up of a commission to investigate the sanitary situation in the colony.[24]

The commission was set up and reported in April 1926. It referred in some detail to the findings of the Rockefeller research team in 1917, and it recommended, among other things, that the International Health Board should be asked to send the staff necessary to work on the plan which had been suggested by the research team. The report of the Public Health Inspector for the year 1926 was issued in August 1927, and it reproduced the researchers' statistics on ankylostomiasis, pointing out that a current survey could have been expected to show a considerable increase in the incidence of infection, so that any public-health campaign against disease generally must first attack hookworm. Later, in November 1928, however, the Governor referred to an outbreak of malaria as having been brought successfully under control, and he noted that the main diseases remaining to be coped with were venereal disease and tuberculosis; he made no mention whatever of ankylostomiasis.[25]

The report of the Acting Chief Medical Officer for 1929 again referred to the continued lack of any action for controlling the spread of ankylostomiasis, which he thought was undoubtably responsible for many cardiac cases and for most of the prevalent anemias. As was by now only to be expected, the report caused no particular comment. The final verdict on the whole problem of ankylostomiasis and the failure to do anything to eradicate it was given some sixteen years after the Rockefeller investigations in a report by the Chief Medical Officer on the medical and sanitary administration in Barbados. He referred to the offers made by the International Health Division of the Rockefeller Foundation to assist with public-health work in Barbados, particularly in connection with hookworm, and mentioned a previous Governor's despair at the apathy of the various Boards. He commented, finally, that "with further study and insight into conditions here, I realized that public health matters are so involved in lay parochial politics and economics and that there is such a complete lack of reciprocity and coordination amongst the separate localities, that to attempt to advise the Government to invite the International Health Division here would not only prove barren, but also ultimately hopelessly embarrassing."[26]

The attempts to introduce measures to control ankylostomiasis had therefore failed. But the light which investigations into this subject had thrown on the whole matter of sanitation generally was to prove of great value in stimulating eventual action. Finally, as a result of the overall improvement in sanitary conditions, a more widespread education in health matters, and the fact that people no longer of necessity went barefoot, hookworm was virtually eradicated.[27] In this way another of the particular disabilities affecting the poor whites was removed.

The effect of the changes in the pattern of emigration, the reforms in education and in the poor relief system that had been initiated in the second half of the nineteenth century, and the eventual reorganisation of public health, began to be shown early in the twentieth century. Nowhere was this more clearly demonstrated than in the area of employment. The poor whites, having achieved educational equality with their black peers, in fact also acquired considerable social advantages. This was particularly evident with respect to employment in the rapidly expanding commercial sector of Bridgetown.

For some time the "Redlegs" had been moving in fair numbers from the country districts into Bridgetown. In 1934 a Barbadian writer drew some interesting "pen pictures of Barbadian life" which provide some indication of their activities and the attitude towards them of the black observer. He described the early developments in the lives of poor whites, once known as "Red-leg Johnnies, Poor Backras, and Scotland Johnnies," and went on to observe: "Many of them have migrated city-wards, and from small beginnings have done so well that they own considerable property in the town. By a thrifty and self-sacrificial mode of living, coupled with a shrewd business acumen, they have contrived to become land and property owners." Among these were the "speculators," largely made up of white Barbadians from the Scotland district: "Johnny . . . having schooled his pedal extremities to the feel of leather or canvas, as the case may be, gathers his earthly possessions which may consist of two and a half goats, and bravely sets out for the Big World [St. Michael] to make his fortune . . . he does this, in a minor way, by methods of trickery, deception, etc."[28]

The larger stores in the centre of Bridgetown were staffed at this time, as indeed to some extent they still are today, almost exclusively by poor whites. Many of them, the children of small rural shopkeepers and fishermen, had been enabled as a result of better educational facilities to obtain employment as "clerks" and "clerkesses," or shop assistants, and, though they might have been, in fact, financially less well off in these circumstances, the move to the city and consequent white-collar employment indicated an improvement in social status. The writer who was previously quoted has left a graphic description of someone termed a "cash boy": "sometimes he is a country boy with red-leg ancestry who has some relative in town and is eager to get some of the gold with which he had heard the streets of Bridgetown are paved. It is not difficult to spot this type of lad: his gait consists of an ambling, shuffling motion with the minimum of arm swing, and for some reason known only to himself the length of his trousers never goes beyond the middle of his shin."

Similarly, in offices and banks, poor whites were very acceptable as employees, once they had had the normal elementary education. An enquiry from the Oversea Resettlement Committee in London elicited the reply from Barbados that there really were no openings in the island since the "number of white people of the clerkly class is more than sufficient to fill all possible vacancies."[29]

Many of these newcomers to the world of commerce made good; some have become the business tycoons of today. The classic example of this success is the Goddard family. There are people still alive today who claim to remember J. N. Goddard, the poor white "speculator," who used to lead his one cow into Bridgetown and there to trade it for what he could get for it. Nevertheless, in 1921 at the age of forty-seven he acquired his own shop in Bridgetown, bought up other businesses, and within the space of twenty-five years owned two large hotels. He was well on the way to establishing a vast business empire and a dynasty not only of tycoons but also of professional men. His nine sons and one daughter were all educated at the island's best schools, several studied abroad, some joined the family firm, one became a medical doctor, one a dancer, and two played cricket for Barbados. The next generation, predictably, are all firmly established in the professions and in business, and some are currently making a considerable contribution to the life of the community.[30]

But though the Goddards present the acme of economic and social mobility, theirs is a pattern which is repeated, on a smaller scale, many times. A detailed survey of this phenomenon lies outside the scope of this study, but suffice it to say that an investigation of the social origins of the inhabitants of the predominantly white middle-class suburban area lying to the east of Bridgetown could be expected to reveal many of poor white or "Redleg" origin.

It is impossible to make any estimate of the numbers of poor whites moving from the country districts into the suburban areas of Christ Church, lying to the east of Bridgetown, or of St. Michael, lying to the west and north of Bridgetown. Nevertheless, such movement is indicated by the fact that, while the overall white population continued to decline, certain parishes showed increases. Christ Church, in particular, increased by about 65 percent between 1911 and 1946, with most of this increase going to the suburban areas of Hastings and Worthing rather than to the rural parts of the parish. St. Michael, excluding Bridgetown, showed a slight increase between 1911 and

Table 4. White Population by Parishes 1911–1946

Parishes	1911	1921	1946
Bridgetown	2,701	1,891	1,385
St. Michael	3,309	3,389	3,563
Christ Church	1,579	1,506	2,473
St. George	411	357	243
St. Philip	891	680	398
St. John	788	715	562
St. James	304	245	318
St. Thomas	290	240	160
St. Joseph	595	483	291
St. Andrew	398	307	124
St. Peter	494	397	236
St. Lucy	303	219	86
Total	12,063	10,429	9,839

Source: Official census reports.

1946, much of which went to the Belleville and Strathclyde areas. St. James increased marginally between 1921 and 1946. But there are no means of identifying statistically the poor whites and other whites in these figures, and since there are no complete emigration figures, these details are of little help except insofar as they provide some confirmation of the move by whites generally from the country into the suburban areas surrounding Bridgetown. It is, however, perhaps worth noting that the total number of people in the three parishes with the highest number of poor whites—St. John, St. Joseph and St. Andrew—dropped from 3,169 in 1871 to 977 in 1946[31] (see Table 4). It is estimated that there are at present no more than a few hundred poor whites in these three parishes.

In any case, many of those who remained in the rural areas had gradually begun improving their position. The fall in sugar prices which began in the mid-nineteenth century led to a number of estates being bought by poor whites who had saved enough money while working as managers and bookkeepers. The senior positions on the plantations had traditionally been filled by persons of poor white descent, but by the second decade of the twentieth century, as a result largely of white emigration, there were more jobs than there were white men to fill them, with the result that many plantation owners had, in the words of a planter from St. Andrew, "reluctantly to resort to coloured men as overseers and book-keepers, which for obvious reasons is not what [they] like or wish to encourage."[32] In fact, at this period much of the skilled and semi-skilled work connected with the plantations was being done by poor whites; they were functioning as blacksmiths, specialist masons dealing with boiling-house furnaces, carters and "horse-doctors." Some, inevitably, remained in the more menial jobs; up to 1940 there were evidently many poor whites working as boiling-house hands in the Scotland district, while as late as 1950 many others were employed in the fields. Indeed, their previous "incapacity" to deal with the hard work of the plantation had become a thing of the past.

It seems that by early in the century the previously high unemployment rate among poor whites had been reduced almost to nothing. For those who remained in the country districts there was always work to be found on the estates, and there was therefore little need to have recourse to poor relief. In St. John, for example, one of the "Guardians of the Poor" reported in 1913 that there were very few applications from poor whites for relief, except for temporary or medical relief in cases of accident or sickness, and that there were at that time only eight white people, who were all very old or crippled, on the permanent pension list.[33]

With the decline in the number of poor whites in the country areas, and their consequent dispersal among much larger numbers of blacks in the city, the traditional pattern of intermarriage gradually began to change. It must be pointed out, however, that the situation was never really as clear-cut as has

The "Redlegs" of Today

(Both by courtesy of Jorgen Bjerre, Aller Press A/S)

been thought. As far back as 1715 the census showed that a handful of white women in St. Philip were married to mulattoes, and a number of mulattoes were listed as having white mothers.[34] Moreover, around the time of Emancipation the rules that were in force for managers on the Drax Hall estate referred to the need to turn off from the military tenements "any white woman who cohabits with a Color'd Man now so common."[35] It was, however, possible that attitudes had hardened after the end of slavery. In any case, in St. Andrew in 1913 there were reported to be only four white men married to black women, three very lower-class white women married to black men, and two white women as having had children for black men.[36] Less than half a century later, however, a close observer of the "Redleg" scene in Barbados, predicting that there would be no more poor whites in existence by the year 2000, cited the large number of mixed marriages as an indication that by that date those who had not joined the white middle class would have become absorbed into the black majority.[37]

The picture of the "Redlegs" during the first half of the twentieth century thus bears remarkably little resemblance to the one which was presented by them little more than a couple of generations before. They retained none but the most superficial reminders of the previous years of degradation and degeneration. Generally speaking, the "Redleg", while he might still be poor, had become reasonably healthy and hardworking and had lost much of his arrogant attitude in his relations with black Barbadians.

Indeed, the commission set up to investigate the labour disturbances of 1937, finding that their causes were fundamentally economic, indicated in no uncertain terms that many types of employment, including those in which the poor whites found themselves, were both extremely underpaid and very badly organised. Clerks and shop assistants, for example, a large proportion of whom were white, were found to be receiving wages which were frequently too low to provide the bare necessities of life, although the conditions and working hours were, in the main, satisfactory. Engineering apprentices and bakers, some of whom were white, were very badly paid with the latter, in particular, frequently working in the most uncomfortable conditions. Peasant farmers, a number of whom would still have been white, were found to be in need of protection, while agricultural labourers were being grossly underpaid. The improvement in conditions resulting from the recommendations of the commission marked, perhaps, the final stage in the rehabilitation of the poor whites.[38]

Conclusion

The factors which combined to provide a solution to the problems posed by the existence of an unemployed and virtually unemployable minority by bringing about, in effect, their gradual disappearance as a class are fairly easily identifiable. Changes in the pattern of emigration and the reforms in education, poor relief and public health, together with the less tangible beginnings of new attitudes towards matters of colour, race and class, had created an entirely new situation in the course of a little over half a century. Not only is there substantial documentary evidence available concerning some aspects of these developments, but there is relevant information in the memories of many of those born around the beginning of this century.

The story of the decline of the indentured servants into poor whites and "Redlegs" is, however, longer and more complex. It has been seen to extend over nearly three centuries, to have been somewhat patchily documented, and to have suffered from the fact that those relating the course of events, or commenting on them, were inevitably subject to a variety of biases. In addition, there are in existence no first-hand accounts provided by the people whose history is being told, except in a few isolated cases of political prisoners in the seventeenth century and in one doubtful case of a poor white woman in the nineteenth century. Nevertheless, it is perhaps worth looking back over the years, now that at least the outline of the pattern of decline has been traced, in an attempt to discover why this decline came about, and the nature of the forces at work in the society which caused this particular sequence of events.

It is necessary first to go back to the original reason for the arrival in Barbados of the indentured servants, whether voluntary or otherwise. They came in order to work as labourers, first to clear the land so that it might be settled and cultivated, then to work on the small estates growing tobacco and cotton and other mixed crops, and then later to provide the labour, in the initial stages, on the bigger and more labour-intensive sugar plantations. Many were induced to come because of the hope of obtaining land—a hope which

115

was very soon to prove unfounded—and many were forced to come because the colonies provided a useful dumping ground for persons who, for political and other reasons, were not wanted in the British Isles. But it was solely the demand for labour that started the stream of emigration. That demand was to disappear, however, soon after the Sugar Revolution of the late 1640s, and with the subsequent introduction of slaves from Africa, there was no longer any need or place for the white labourer. Thus it was little more than twenty years after the first permanent settlement of Barbados had been effected that the process of decline of the white labouring class had set in.

It would, of course, have been too much at that particular time to expect the authorities either in England or Barbados to recognise the fact that this category of persons no longer had any significant role to play in the economy of the island, and thus to take steps to limit the immigration of white labourers into Barbados. indeed, the Barbadians did exactly the reverse, and when the stream of immigrants had dwindled to a trickle after 1660, they made every effort to persuade the Council for Foreign Plantations in London to send them more servants. They did not, as has been seen, give up the struggle until the end of the seventeenth century, when it had already been obvious for several years that the sources of supply of white servants, for Barbados, at least, had dried up.

The reasons for this apparently illogical sequence of events are not far to seek. As far as the English were concerned, although after 1660 attempts were made to rationalise the arrangements for transportation to the colonies, the detailed requirements of the various colonies for manpower were not considered. Barbados, in any case, was only one of the colonies for which emigrants were leaving, and the competition offered both by other areas in the Caribbean with more land available, and by mainland America with its more familiar climate as well as exceedingly large tracts of land, was soon to prove too great for the island. The laws of supply and demand came into play, causing a decrease in the number of white people reaching Barbados. This happened, however, rather later than would have been the case had any thought been given to the matter of relating the supply of manpower to the needs of the local economy.

In the case of Barbados, the motives of the Assembly, which was composed at that time almost exclusively of planters, are fairly clear. The planters were above all motivated by self-interest. They had become extremely rich within the course of a few years and were concerned with preserving what they possessed. Once having acquired a near sufficiency of cheap and relatively efficient slave labour to work on the plantations, it would not have occurred to them to interest themselves in the employment prospects and welfare of their former servants, whom they had paid off at the end of their periods of indenture. On the other hand, the planters were extremely anxious to keep up the level of the white population, since, in spite of the store they set by their identity as Barbadians, they still regarded the island as an English settlement and were acutely aware of the potential threat offered to their security by the increasing number of African slaves who were being imported each year into Barbados.

The greater the number of white inhabitants, of whatever class, the better their chances of suppressing any disaffection on the part of the slaves, and the more adequate also their protection against a foreign aggressor, although, given the lack of attention paid over the years both to the physical defence of the island and the training of the Militia, this was evidently not an overriding consideration. What was unmistakably clear was that the question of an economic basis for the continuing existence of a large white population was of little or no concern to them.

This total lack of concern not only with the opportunities for employment but also with the other aspects of the welfare of the indentured servants and poor whites as a class, let alone as individuals, could be seen operating in the attitudes of the Assembly even into the twentieth century. In the eighteenth and nineteenth centuries, however, given the prevailing contemporary metropolitan attitudes towards the poor, it could hardly have been otherwise. While the duty of the rich was admittedly to be benevolent, the business of the poor was to be industrious; and if they were not so, then abject poverty was inescapable in this life, with the possibility of salvation only in another life. The poor whites of Barbados generally, it has been demonstrated, hardly fell into the category of industrious, and therefore deserving, poor.

Evidently the Barbadian planters had not only transported to the colony many of the worst features of English life, but, as is the case with colonists generally, they had even exaggerated those features and maintained them long after things in the home country had changed for the better. On the other hand, various governors sent out from England were regularly engaged in trying to persuade the Barbadians to introduce reforms. From Tufton in 1629, who was appalled by the cruelty with which the planters treated their servants, through Dutton in 1681 and Kendall in 1691 (both of whom tried unsuccessfully to persuade the Assembly that legislation was needed to protect servants from ill treatment by their masters), to the governors concerned with major reforms in the nineteenth century, the pattern remained the same. Thus it was that the suggestions by Governor Reid for improving the employment situation of the poor whites remained unremarked by the Assembly, and Governor Hincks' schemes for their resettlement elsewhere in the Caribbean were initially frustrated by the Assemblies not only of Barbados but also of St. Vincent. Thus it was also that Pope Hennessy was from the start unacceptable in Barbados owing to the complete incompatibility of his reforming zeal with the hide-bound conservatism of the Barbadian planters. And thus it was that two successive governors in the 1920s attempted but totally failed to break through the resistance of the Assembly and the vestries to the introduction of a campaign to eradicate hookworm, something which would have been of immeasurable benefit not only to the poor white sector of the population but to the poorer classes generally.

Inevitably, the attitudes of the Assembly and the planters were of prime importance as far as the welfare of the poor whites was concerned. They revealed themselves, however, in a mainly negative sense—through activities that were not undertaken, essential measures that were not introduced, or obstacles that were put in the way of reforms—rather than any positive actions or statements concerning the poor whites. Even the Poor Relief Commission's report of 1878, despite its frank acknowledgement of the situation of the poor whites, totally failed to make any recommendations about action to improve their position. However, it was more frequently in the comments and criticisms of private individuals that the true attitudes of higher status whites towards the poor whites were to emerge unequivocally. A reformer like Joshua Steele, for example, leaves no room for doubt about his view of the poor whites as morally degenerate; nevertheless, he was prepared to make an effort towards their rehabilitation and even succeeded in getting legislation through the Assembly. J. W. Orderson, a little later, was very much in the same category. But neither, as far as can be seen, succeeded in achieving any positive results. Influential opinion was evidently weighted too heavily against them.

The observations made by visitors to Barbados reflected much the same kinds of attitudes, most of which were then current, or had until recently been current, in the metropole. The poverty of the poor whites, they suggested, was caused by something inherent in the people themselves; it was some lack of moral fiber that had brought them to this pass; it was perhaps even some misconduct in their past which had brought its retribution by reducing them to the level of the blacks. It was believed that one of the indications of the lack of moral fiber was their addiction to rum, with its predictably dire consequences, a belief that reflected, no doubt, the awareness of the harm that cheap gin had done to mid-eighteenth century London slum dwellers until its sale had been restricted by legislation. Moreover, the tendency of some of these writers to compare the poor whites with the blacks greatly to the advantage of the latter again reflected to some extent attitudes which were then current in England. But this may have been partly due to the culture shock of seeing, in a colonial territory, white people living at the same impoverished level as blacks. It may also have been due to the tendency among eighteenth-century intellectuals to embrace the concept of the black man as a "noble savage." By the latter part of the century, some 5 percent of the population of London was black, and there was, in fact, comparatively little racial prejudice, as the term is understood today, until well on into the nineteenth century.

The inescapable fact of the poor whites' existence was that they formed a class which had no economic role to play, and thus employers of labour, whether in the town or the country, were not disposed to make any adjustments to accommodate them. It was only to be expected therefore that the more energetic and ambitious among them would seize whatever means was available of escaping from their virtually untenable situation, whether by emigration or otherwise. It was certain, however, that many of them were incapable of so doing; years of frustration, ill treatment, malnutrition, unsanitary living conditions, and disease had all taken their toll. Hampered by both their physical circumstances and psychological outlook, scorned both by other whites and by blacks, their own attitudes militated strongly against them, forcing them into a position from which at the time there seemed to be no escape.

The poor whites proved unacceptable to higher status whites on account both of their total unwillingness to work and their special arrogance. Had they been industrious, they would no doubt have fallen into the category of deserving poor and experienced some form of benevolence from the rich. They were very markedly, however, not industrious. They were not prepared to do any work of the kind generally available to them since it was of a type done only by blacks. They were not even prepared to branch out into new activities that were specially geared to their own presumed capabilities, such as were provided for them by Joshua Steele's plans for encouraging spinning, weaving and the like. At the same time, however, they were peculiarly arrogant. This feature, which struck visitors so forcibly, made them even more unacceptable at a time when the poor were supposed to "know their place" and to be, in addition to being industrious, both subservient and grateful for any small mercies which might come their way.

Their nonacceptance by higher status whites might have been of much less significance had they themselves been prepared to accept the fact that their position, at least after Emancipation and to some extent before it, was equivalent economically and socially to that of the blacks among whom they lived. As their attitude to work indicated, this they stubbornly refused to do. They regarded themselves as indisputably superior to the blacks solely because of their white skins. Not only would they not work on equal terms with blacks, but they did not wish to be educated with them or mix with them socially, much less marry with them. Very likely these attitudes hardened considerably after Emancipation. During the period of slavery, however, when the poor white might have felt justified as a free man in considering himself superior to the black slave, there was evidence of sexual relationships, including marriage, between poor whites and free coloureds.

The attitude of the blacks towards the poor whites is more difficult to define. There were examples around the turn of the eighteenth century of atrocities perpetrated by poor whites on blacks, but there were also references to charitable acts done to poor whites by the slaves. No doubt there was generally little love lost between the two groups. In fact, given the situation at the time when the norm was for the white man to be always in a position of superiority over the black man, the latter would certainly despise the poor white for falling not only well below the level of others of his own colour but also below the economic level of the blacks themselves. This, in turn, cannot but have tended to confirm the poor white in his originally self-inflicted isolation.

But while the underlying reason for the decline of the poor whites was an economic one, there was another important factor to be taken into consideration. This was the physical environment. The fundamental difference between the original environment of the poor whites and their adopted one was that of climate. Contrary to the views expressed in some quarters, it seems unlikely that it was this that prevented the white man from working in the fields. As was pointed out in the debate on the subject which took place at the turn of the eighteenth century, the original English settlement of Barbados had been carried out by white men. It was after the introduction of the slaves, while white men still continued to spend many hours in the sun superintending the work on the estates, that the idea took shape that white men were incapable of working as agricultural labourers. The conclusion to-day would seem to be that the white man, given a period of acclimatisation and appropriate diet and clothing, is at no particular disadvantage when working, in whatever capacity, in a tropical climate. Hence the real significance of the effect of the climate on the poor white must be sought elsewhere. The fact was that the climate made it possible for him to subsist without working in a way which would have been impossible for an Englishman of an equivalent class living in a temperate climate. The poor white of Barbados had no need to bother unduly about housing and clothing, and not at all about heating; and while he had to concern himself to some extent about food, with a little exertion he could almost live off the land. The fact that the climate in Barbados made life comparatively easy for the poor white, and that he did not have to struggle for his existence, as did his English cousins, was one important contributory factor in determining his overall decline.

During the two and a half centuries or so that no particular regard was paid to their situation, it was only those "Redlegs" of exceptional calibre who were able to escape from their downward spiral. As soon, however, as attitudes towards the socially underprivileged changed and it was realised that exceptional measures had to be introduced to deal with the problems affecting a specific class, then a new pattern began to emerge. As soon also as poor whites were forced, through the removal of any special status, to mix on equal terms with their black peers, then much of their former arrogance began, albeit slowly, to disappear, and their relationship with the rest of the community placed on a more realistic footing. The proof of this lies in the fact that there is no longer a "Redleg" problem in Barbados and that this class within the next generation or two will have become nothing more than a curious, if not almost forgotten, historical phenomenon.

Notes

Introduction

1. J. H. Sutton Moxly, *An Account of a West Indian Sanatorium and a Guide to Barbados* (London, 1886), p. 128.
2. Frank A. Collymore, *Notes for A Glossary of Words and Phrases of Barbadian Dialect,* 4th ed., rev. and enl. (Bridgetown, Barbados: Advocate Co. Ltd., 1970), p. 44.
3. Barbados Statistical Service, *Preliminary Bulletin on the Population Census of 1970,* gives the total white population as 9354, the total black population as 215,204 and the total population as 235,229.
4. Mr. Trevor Marshall, of the University of the West Indies, kindly provided the text of this song. The programme was presented at the Barbados Museum on 22 February 1974.
5. Presented by the Barbados Writers' Workshop in August 1972.
6. Lionel Hutchinson, *One Touch of Nature* (London: Collins, 1971).
7. *Oxford English Dictionary* (ed. 1933).
8. J. Graham Cruikshank, "Negro English, with reference particularly to Barbados," *Timehri,* 3d. ser. 1 (January 1911).
9. See, for example, Edward A. Stoute, "The 'Poor Whites' of Barbados," *The Bajan,* no. 218 (November 1971).
10. J. W. Williamson, *Medical and miscellaneous observations relative to the West India Islands* (Edinburgh: 1817), p. 27. The Scotland district is shown by most cartographers as lying in the eastern part of St. Andrew and extending some way into St. Joseph. According to the current definition, given in the Soil Conservation (Scotland District) Act, 1958, it extends along the coast from Pico Teneriffe to Consett Point and inland roughly as far as the boundary of the coral cap.
11. Nathaniel Hawthorne, ed., *Yarn of a Yankee Privateer* (New York: Funk and Wagnalls Co., 1926), p. 138.
12. Joseph Sturge and Thomas Harvey, *The West Indies in 1837,* p. 380; J. A.

Thome and J. H. Kimball, *Emancipation in the West Indies*, p. 282.

13. "Journal of John Bowen Colthurst, July 1835 to August 1838," Boston Public Library, Boston, Mass. Dr. Woodville Marshall, of the University of the West Indies, kindly allowed me to consult his typescript of this manuscript. See p. 65 for illustration.

14. John Davy, *The West Indies before and since Slave Emancipation*, p. 68.

15. Minutes of Assembly (1872-1873), app. A, p. 8.

16. N. Darnell Davis, *Cavaliers and Roundheads of Barbados*, p. 83.

17. *Report of West India Royal Commission* (1897), app. C, pt. 1(6).

18. Patrick Leigh Fermor, *Travellers' Tree* (London: John Murray, 1950), pp. 137-138.

19. Nicholas Monsarrat, *Life is a Four-Letter Word*, book II. (London: Pan Books Ltd., 1972), pp. 341-342.

20. Calendar of State Papers (1675-1676), No. 812.

21. Property qualifications for franchise, in existence since the early days of settlement, were codified in an act of 18 July 1721 (Richard Hall, *Acts passed in the Island of Barbados*, pp. 252-269). They were not modified in such a way as to have any effect on poor whites until the act of 6 June 1840 (*Public Acts* (1830-1837), 3 Vict. no. 29, pp. 232-259).

22. *Minutes of Assembly* (1877-1878), app. B. p. 92.

Chapter 1

1. A factor making for confusion over dates is the use in England until 1751 of the Julian, rather than the Gregorian calendar. The Julian year ended on 24 March and the new year began on 25 March, and thus the date of the landing appears in contemporary documents as February 1626. Throughout this study dates are transposed to conform with modern usage.

2. G. T. Barton, *Prehistory of Barbados* (Bridgetown: Advocate Press, 1953), summarises the available evidence.

3. This incident was originally believed to have occurred in 1605, which is the date inscribed on the monument at Holetown commemorating the event. It has, however, been shown conclusively in J. A. Williamson's *Caribbee Islands under the Proprietary Patents* (London: OUP, 1926) that 1605 was a compiler's error for 1625.

4. V. T. Harlow, *History of Barbados*, p. 3, quoting *Memoirs of the First Settlement* (Barbados, 1741), p. 1. Harlow's work should in any case be consulted for further details of this period.

5. Carl and Roberta Bridenbaugh, *No Peace beyond the Line*, pp. 35-38.

6. Captain John Smith, *True Travels, Adventures and Observations*, pp. 55-56.

7. Harlow, *History*, quoting various sources.

8. Ibid., p. 4, quoting Trinity College Dublin MSS G.4.15, no. 736, pp. 157-163.
9. Shaftesbury Papers, PRO/30/24/49, f. 2b.
10. Harlow, *Colonising Expeditions to the West Indies and Guiana* (London: Haklyut Society, 1925), p. 37, quoting Rawlinson MSS 'C' 94.
11. Egerton MSS 2395, f. 602.
12. Davis, *Cavaliers and Roundheads*, pp. 32-33, quoting the Winthrop Papers.
13. Ibid., p. 38.
14. A. P. Newton, *European Nations in the West Indies* (London: A. and C. Black, 1933), p. 157. The rivalry between Sir William Courteen and the Earl of Carlisle was an important factor bedevilling the potentially progressive development of the island in its early years. Although Courteen's men had staked the first claim to the island, the Earl of Carlisle had succeeded in obtaining from Charles I a formal grant of the Caribbee Islands, including Barbados, in July 1627. Courteen, through his friend the Earl of Pembroke, subsequently was able, in February 1628, to obtain a grant of several islands, also including Barbados. Protracted negotiations resulted in Pembroke's claim being nullified in May 1629; Barbados thus remained under the proprietorship of the Earl of Carlisle. Nevertheless, in spite of the complications resulting from the existence of opposing groups of settlers, Barbados seems to have had a fairly promising first two years or so of its existence as an English settlement. Harlow, *History*, pp. 7-13, contains further relevant details.
15. Smith, *True Travels*, pp. 55-56, and for subsequent extracts.
16. Shaftesbury Papers, PRO/30/24/49, f. 2b.
17. "The Voyage of Sir Henry Colt Knight to the Iland of the Antilles," extract in *BMHS Journal* XXI, no. 1 (November 1953): 7.
18. Harlow, *History*, p. 6; Egerton MSS 2395, f. 602; Newton, *European Nations*, p. 157.
19. Richard S. Dunn, *Sugar and Slaves*, p. 55.
20. Carl Bridenbaugh, *Vexed and Troubled Englishmen*, p. 469.
21. J. C. Hotten, *Original Lists of Persons of Quality and Others who Emigrated to America*, pp. 38-142, 296-297, 300.
22. N. Darnell Davis Papers, Box 2, Env. 39.
23. Bridenbaugh, *Vexed and Troubled*, p. 418.
24. F. P. Verney, *Memoirs of the Verney Family during the Civil War* (London, 1892), vol. 1, p. 154.
25. Hotten, *Original Lists*, pp. 296-297.
26. Davis Papers, Box 1, Env. 27.
27. Davis, *Cavaliers and Roundheads*, pp. 32-33, quoting the Winthrop Papers.
28. Davis Papers, Box 7, Env. 22.
29. Bridenbaugh, *No Peace*, p. 37, quoting *Memoirs of the Verney Family*.

30. Davis Papers, Box 1, Env. 7.
31. Davis, *Cavaliers and Roundheads,* p. 71; *Present State of the West Indies* (London, 1778), p. 65.
32. Thomasson Tracts, 669, f. 11(115).
33. Davis Papers, Box 7, Env. 22.
34. John Bruce, ed. *Letters and Papers of the Verney Family* (London, 1853), p. 194.
35. Alan Burns, *History of the British West Indies,* p. 223; Harlow, *History,* p. 14.
36. Davis Papers, Box 7, Env. 22.
37. "Voyage of Sir Henry Colt," *BMHS Journal* XXI, no. 1 (November 1953): 7.
38. Andrew White, *Narrative of a Voyage to Maryland,* (Baltimore: Maryland Historical Society, 1874), p. 15.
39. Bridenbaugh, *No Peace,* pp. 22-23.

Chapter 2

1. Richard Ligon, *True and Exact History of Barbados,* p. 110.
2. "Servants to Foreign Plantations from Bristol, England to Barbados, 1654-1686," *BMHS Journal* XIV, nos. 1 & 2, 3 & 4; XV, no. 4; XVI, nos. 1, 2 & 3; XVII, nos. 2 & 3; XVIII, nos. 1, 2, 3 & 4; XIX, no. 1; extracted from Tolzey Books in Bristol.
3. Aubrey Gwynn, "Cromwell's Policy of Transportation," *Studies—an Irish Quarterly Review* XIX, no. 76 (December 1930): 608.
4. Additional MSS 11411, f. 9.
5. Oliver Cromwell, *Oliver Cromwell's Letters and Speeches with Elucidations by Thomas Carlyle,* Vol. I. (New York, 1845), p. 383. *CSP* (1574-1660), pp. 421, 427-428. Later, in 1655, Cromwell appears to have initiated a clearing out of the prisoners; the soldiers taken earlier at Dunbar and held in Tynemouth Castle were to be sent to Barbados along with those captured in the Brest man-of-war and committed to the Marshalsea, and the English, Irish and Dutch mariners who were prisoners in the Castle of Plymouth and were not thought fit to be tried for their lives.
6. Cromwell, *Letters and Speeches,* vol. II, pp. 164-165.
7. L. F. Stock, ed., *Proceedings and Debates of the British Parliaments respecting North America,* vol. I. (Washington, D. C., 1924-1941), pp. 247-350.
8. Lucas Transcripts, *Minutes of Council,* vol. I, p. 214.
9. *CSP* (1574-1660), pp. 419, 447.

10. J. J. Williams, *Whence the "Black Irish" of Jamaica?* (New York: Dial Press Inc., 1932), p. 12.

11. Robert Dunlop, *Ireland under the Commonwealth*, vol. II. (Manchester, 1913), pp. 477, 549.

12. Abbott Emerson Smith, *Colonists in Bondage*, p. 71.

13. Ibid., p. 143.

14. *CSP* (1574-1660), pp. 457-458.

15. Ligon, *History*, p. 13.

16. Henry Whistler, "Journal of the West India Expedition," extract in *BMHS Journal* V, no. 4, (August 1938): 185.

17. John Jennings, *Acts and Statutes of the Island of Barbados*, pp. 15-16.

18. "Servants to Foreign Plantations," *BMHS Journal* XV, no. 4 (August 1948): p. 216.

19. Harlow, *Colonising Expeditions*, p. 44.

20. Ligon, *History*, pp. 44-45, 109, 113.

21. Jennings, *Acts*, items 7-11, 30, 39, 62, 72.

22. Ligon, *History*, pp. 45-46. Curiously enough, in spite of the fact that both the context and the terminology of this passage make it quite clear that servants and not black slaves are involved, at least a dozen subsequent historians and others, starting with Oldmixon and including Poyer and Schomburgk, have referred to the incident as a conspiracy of Negro slaves. Indeed, any doubt about this could have been removed by reference to the legislation resulting from this incident. An Act was passed, on 4 October 1649, instituting a Council of War, "for the trial of persons guilty of the late Insurrection of Servants," and another, on 15 November 1649, for "an annual day of Thanksgiving for our deliverance from the late Insurrection" which, as was explained in a note, referred to the recent rebellion of servants. Hall, *Acts*, p. 461, gives the titles but no texts. For a more detailed account of this incident and its various misinterpretations see Jill Sheppard, "The Slave Conspiracy that Never Was" *BMHS Journal* XXXIV, no. 4, (March 1974): pp. 190-197.

23. Hall, *Acts*, p. 450, no text.

24. "Expedition of Penn and Venables to the West Indies," Lucas Transcripts, *Miscellaneous*, vol. V, p. 342.

25. Lucas Transcripts, *Minutes of Council*, vol. I, pp. 368, 372-375.

26. *CSP* (1574-1660), p. 481.

27. *CSP* (1665-1668), no. 1657.

28. A. D. Chandler, "Expansion of Barbados" *BMHS Journal* XIII, nos. 3 & 4, (March-October 1946): 114.

29. Harlow, *History*, p. 117.

30. Thomas Birch, ed., *Collection of the State Papers of John Thurloe*, vol. V. (London, 1742), p. 652.

31. Chandler, "Expansion of Barbados," p. 114.

32. Dunn, *Sugar and Slaves*, pp. 75-76.

Chapter 3

1. Dunn, *Sugar and Slaves*, pp. 80-83. It should be noted that in this description Dunn is comparing Barbados with the other colonies in America and the Caribbean. He admits that in the 1660s and 1670s the Barbados planters were no longer as rich as they had been.
2. *CSP* (1665-1668), no. 1657.
3. "A Prospect of Bridgetown in Barbados," a copper plate engraving in the Barbados Museum. See p. 26 for illustration.
4. *CSP* (1574-1660), p. 492.
5. *CSP* (1661-1668), no. 802.
6. *CSP* (1675-1676, addenda 1574-1675), no. 1214.
7. Michael Ghirelli, *Emigrants from England to America 1682-1692*, pp. 95-96.
8. *CSP* (1661-1668), no. 772.
9. "Servants to Foreign Plantations," see Chapter II, note 2.
10. Ghirelli, *Emigrants*.
11. J. C. Jeaffreson, *A Young Squire of the Seventeenth Century from the Papers (Ad 1676-1686) of Christopher Jeaffreson* (London, 1878).
12. Lucas Transcripts, *Minutes of Council*, vol. 2, p. 207.
13. Smith, *Colonists*, pp. 181, 184-185.
14. Hotten, *Original Lists*, pp. 313-342.
15. CO 30/5, ff. 156-160.
16. Hall, *Acts*, p. 484.
17. T. B. Macaulay, *History of England* (London, 1889), pp. 317-318. Macaulay's John Cod is presumably John Coad, who related his experiences in *A Memorandum of the Wonderful Providence of God to a poor unworthy Creature, during the time of the Duke of Monmouth's Rebellion and the Revolution of 1688* (London, 1849).
18. Henry Pitman, *A Relation of the great sufferings and strange adventures of Henry Pitman, Chirurgeon to the late Duke of Monmouth* (London, 1689), pp. 11-12.
19. *CSP* (1689-1692), nos. 700, 968, 1184, 1193.
20. Richard Rawlin, *The Laws of Barbados*, pp. 176-177.
21. *CSP* (1661-1668), no. 858.
22. CO 1/44, no. 47, ff. 141-379; Dunn, *Sugar and Slaves*, whose total figures have been used.
23. *CSP* (1661-1668), nos. 85, 578.
24. *CSP* (1661-1668), nos. 24, 324, 764.
25. *CSP* (1669-1674), no. 549.
26. Davis, *Cavaliers and Roundheads*, pp. 83-84.
27. Harlow, *History*, p. 152.
28. *CSP* (1661-1668), no. 528.

29. *CSP* (1661-1668), no. 1657; *CSP* (1689-1692), no. 771.
30. See note 21.
31. Chandler, *Expánsion of Barbados*, pp. 124-134.
32. Dunn, *Sugar and Slaves*, pp. 75-76.
33. *CSP* (1669-1674), no. 1101.
34. Dunn, *Sugar and Slaves*, pp. 87-88.
35. *CSP* (1689-1692), no. 1034.
36. *CSP* (1697-1698), no. 52.
37. *CSP* (1675-1676), nos. 682, 690.
38. *CSP* (1685-1688), no. 579; *Minutes of Council*, 16 February 1686.
39. *CSP* (1689-1692), no. 2599.
40. *CSP* (1701), nos. 1112, 1190.
41. *CSP* (1669-1674), no. 1098; *CSP* (1689-1692), no. 1034.
42. CO 29/1, pp. 70-71.
43. Stowe MSS 755, f. 119.
44. *CSP* (1669-1674), no. 501; *CSP* (1675-1676), no. 682; *CSP* (1677-1680), no. 969; *CSP* (1681-1685), no. 1195; Lucas Transcripts, *Minutes of Council*, vol. VI, pp. 4, 6.
45. *CSP* (1689-1697), no. 1108; Lucas Transcripts, *Minutes of Council*, vol. VI, p. 17.
46. *CSP* (1696-1697), nos. 620, 657.
47. CO 28/3, f. 44.
48. CO 30/6, Acts of 29 November 1698.
49. CO 30/6, Acts of 1 February, 18 and 26 May, 2 August 1699; 27 February 1700.
50. CO 28/6, f. 82. For a more detailed account of this incident see Jill Sheppard, "The Sojourn in Barbados of Two Thousand Disbanded Soldiers," *BMHS Journal* XXXV, no. 2, (March 1976): pp. 138-143.
51. Hall, *Acts*, pp. 35-42.
52. William Belgrove, A *Treatise upon husbandry or planting*, (Boston, 1755), and Lascelles and others, *Instructions for the management of plantations in Barbados* (London, 1786), include Sir Henry Drax's instructions, without dating them. It seems likely that the reference is to the Henry Drax who died in 1684.
53. *CSP* (1681-1685), nos. 59, 250.
54. Lucas Transcripts, *Minutes of Council*, vol. V, pp. 14-15.
55. CO 30/6, Act of 17 November 1701.
56. *CSP* (1703), no. 1110.
57. CO 30/5, Acts of 10 August 1682, 17 November 1701, and 1 December 1703.
58. *CSP* (1693-1696), no. 1738.
59. *CSP* (1693-1696), no. 1738; *CSP* (1661-1668), no. 1347; *CSP* (1669-1674), nos. 357, 413.

60. *CSP* (1669-1674), no. 357.
61. Bridenbaugh, *No Peace*, p. 281.
62. CO 30/2.
63. *CSP* (1669-1674), no. 562.
64. Rawlin, *Laws*, p. 148.
65. *CSP* (1697-1698), no. 52.

Chapter 4

1. *CSP* (1712-1714), no. 45.
2. *CSP* (1714-1715), nos. 534 and 548.
3. CO 28/16.
4. *CSP* (1714-1715), no. 654.
5. Hall, *Acts*, pp. 138-155.
6. *CSP* (1734-1735), nos. 1, 137 and 257.
7. *CSP* (1697-1698), no. 22.
8. *CSP* (1738), no. 494.
9. Population figures from E. B. Burley, *Memorandum summarising the returns of the census taken in the Island of Barbados in the year 1715* (Barbados, 1913), published in the *Official Gazette*, 14 November 1913, pp. 1677-1692.
10. Figures from lists in J. and M. Kaminkov, *List of Emigrants from England to America 1718-1759* (Baltimore: Magna Carta Book Co., 1964).
11. Figures from lists in J. and M. Kaminkov, *Original Lists of Emigrants in Bondage from London to the American Colonies 1719-1744* (Baltimore: Magna Carta Book Co., 1967).
12. "Prisoners of the '45 Rising," *BMHS Journal* XXX, no. 2, (May 1963): 73-90.
13. "John Poyer's Letter to Lord Seaforth," *BMHS Journal* VIII, no. 4, (August 1941): 161-162.
14. Additional MSS 43507, ff. 1-5.
15. Belgrove, *Treatise*.
16. Hall, *Acts*, pp. 378-379.
17. Lascelles and others, *Instructions*, pp. 19-20.
18. Richard Hall, *General Account of the first settlement and of the trade and Constitution of the island of Barbados, written in the year 1755*, (Barbados, 1924), p. 8.
19. John Poyer, *History of Barbados*, pp. 379-399; Samuel Moore, *Public Acts in force ...* , pp. 212-217.
20. William Dickson, *Letters on Slavery* (London, 1789), p. 41.
21. Harry Bennett, Jr., *Bondsmen and Bishops—Slavery and Apprenticeship on the Codrington Plantations of Barbados 1710-1838* (Berkeley: University of California Press, 1958), p. 36.

22. *Barbados Mercury*, 15 December 1818.
23. *Barbados Mercury*, 7 September 1822.
24. *Society for the Encouragement of Arts, Manufactures and Commerce in Barbados; Institution and First Proceedings of the Society 1781-1784* (Barbados, 1784), p. 37.
25. St. Michael Vestry Minute Books, 10 March and 4 August 1783.
26. *Barbadian*, 14 January 1857.
27. Burley, *Memorandum;* Handler and Sio in their contribution "Barbados" to David W. Cohen and Jack P. Greene, eds., *Neither Slave nor Free* (Baltimore: Johns Hopkins University Press, 1972), confirm this figure.
28. Edward Eliot, *Christianity and Slavery; in a course of lectures preached at the Cathedral and Parish Church of St. Michael, Barbados* (London, 1833), pp. 225-226.
29. Dickson, *Letters*, pp. 57-58.
30. Lucas Transcripts, *Minutes of Council*, vol. 32, pp. 116-117.
31. CO 28/71, despatches 45 and 48 of 1 September and 13 November 1804.
32. Richard Towne, *Treatise of the diseases most frequent in the West Indies, and herein more particularly of those which occur in Barbados* (London, 1726), pp. 114-115, 188.
33. Rev. Griffith Hughes, *Natural History of Barbados* (London, 1750), pp. 35-36.
34. Lucas Transcripts, *Minutes of Council*, vol. 31, p. 83.
35. William Dickson, *Mitigation of Slavery* (London, 1814), p. 155.
36. Dickson, *Letters*, p. 41.
37. Daniel McKinnen, *Tour through the British West Indies in the Years 1802 and 1803* (London, 1805), pp. 30-31.
38. R. R. Madden, *Twelvemonth's Residence in the West Indies* (London, 1835), pp. 40-41.
39. See Introduction.
40. H. J. Chapman, *Barbados and other Poems* (London, 1833), p. 27. F. A. Hoyos has an interesting note on Chapman in *BMHS Journal*, XVI nos. 1 & 2, (November 1948-February 1949): 14-20.
41. George Pinckard, *Notes on the West Indies* (London, 1806), pp. 132-139.
42. H. N. Coleridge, *Six Months in the West Indies in 1825* (London, 1832), p. 305.
43. F. W. N. Bayley, *Four Years' Residence in the West Indies* (London, 1830), p. 62.
44. Sturge and Harvey, *West Indies*, p. 380.
45. Thomas Rolph, *Brief Account together with Observations made during a visit in the West Indies* (Dundas, 1836), pp. 48-49.
46. *Barbados Mercury*, 28 September 1822.
47. *Barbadian*, 24 February 1836.
48. St. John Vestry, 6 February 1654; 25 June 1655; 2 March 1656 and 16 October 1657.

49. Will dated 17 February 1662 in recopied Wills Book.
50. Rawlin, *Laws,* p. 116; St. John Vestry, 21 December 1681.
51. *Minutes of Assembly,* 9 July and 26 November 1776; the "fruits" mentioned are probably those of the sea grape (Coccoloba uvifera), which is to be found on most of the beaches of Barbados.
52. Lucas Transcripts, *Minutes of Council,* vol. 32, p. 33.
53. *Minutes of Assembly,* 30 June and 28 July 1812.
54. Original Act of 26 September 1826.
55. *Barbadian,* 7 November 1835; 7 March 1838; 9 October 1839.
56. Will dated 4 December 1679 in recopied Wills Book.
57. J. Oldmixon, *British Empire in America* (London, 1708), vol. II, p. 101.
58. Lucas Transcripts, *Misc.,* vol. II, pp. 306-312, 362-416.
59. *CSP* (1704-1705), no. 1251; *CSP* (1707), no. 697; *CSP* (1719-1720), no. 356.
60. Lucas Transcripts, *Misc.,* vol. II, pp. 362-416.
61 . H. N. Haskell, "Some Notes on the Foundation and History of Harrison College," *BMHS Journal* VIII, no. 4, (August 1941): 192-193; and IX, no. 1, (November 1941): 2-9.
62. Frank J. Klingberg, *Codrington Chronicle—an experiment in Anglican Altruism on a Barbados Plantation 1710-1834* (Berkeley: University of California Press, 1949), p. 110.
62. Bennett, *Bondsmen,* pp. 5 & 9.
64. Lucas Transcripts, *Misc.,* Index, p. 2.
65. P. A. Farrar, "Christ Church Foundation School," *BMHS Journal* VIII, no. 2 (February 1941): 69.
66. Robert H. Schomburgk, *History of Barbados,* pp. 104.
67. *Public Acts, 1800-1829,* pp. 119-124.
68. St. John Vestry, 14 May 1792; 25 November 1807.
69. Schomburgk, *History,* p. 106.
70. St. Philip Vestry, 25 March 1808; 14 March 1832; Blue Book, 1833.
71. *Barbadian,* 30 March 1839.
72. St. Philip Vestry, 9 February 1808.
73. J. W. Orderson, *Leisure Hours at the Pier: Or, a Treatise on the Education of the Poor of Barbados* (Liverpool, 1827).
74. Burley, *Memorandum;* Thome and Kimball, *Emancipation,* p. 230.

Chapter 5

1. Hall, *Acts,* pp. 460, 461, 463 (titles only).
2. Ligon, *History,* p. 100.
3. Harlow, *History,* p. 71.
4. Poyer, *History,* p. 59.
5. Jennings, *Acts and Statutes,* pp. 77-78; 116-125.

6. Harlow, *History*, p. 81.

7. Birch, ed., *State Papers of John Thurloe*, vol. 5, p. 564; *CSP* (1661-1668), no. 1788.

8. Hall, *Acts*, p. 472 (title only).

9. *CSP* (1669-1674), no. 1098.

10. *CSP* (1661-1668), no. 1657.

11. Hall, *Acts*, pp. 466-468, 473, 475-476 (titles only) give an indication of the types of amendments to the existing laws.

12. CO 32/2, ff. 89-93.

13. Hall, *Acts*, p. 477 (title only).

14. CO 30/2, ff. 133-151, which gives the date as 15 April 1682; the title given by Hall is, however, dated 1680, which seems to be confirmed both by the sequence of laws in CO 30/2 and the references in subsequent legislation.

15. Hall, *Acts*, pp. 138-155.

16. *CSP* (1703), no. 787.

17. CO 30/6, ff. 158-159; CO 30/15, act. no. 125.

18. Lucas Transcripts, *Minutes of Council*, vol. 24, p. 490.

19. *Minutes of Assembly*, 12 August 1739.

20. See, for example, King's MSS 205, ff. 456-473; Lucas Transcripts, *Minutes of Council*, vol. 28, pp. 56, 209; and *Minutes of Assembly*, 1 October 1776.

21. N. A. T. Hall, "Study of Constitutional and Political Developments in Barbados and Jamaica 1783-1815" (unpublished Ph.D. thesis), quoting *Minutes of Assembly*, 14 January 1794.

22. *Minutes of Assembly*, 29 April 1783.

23. Ibid., 15 March 1787.

24. Burley, *Memorandum*.

25. Lucas Transcripts, *Minutes of Council*, vol. 31, pp. 408-409;Original Act.

26. Samuel Moore, *Public Acts in Force ... from 11th May 1762 to April 8th 1800 inclusive*, pp. 381, 408.

27. *Minutes of Assembly*, 7 March 1805.

28. Ibid., 8 October 1816.

29. Original Act.

30. Original Act.

31. Original Act.

32. *Barbadian*, 4 December 1841.

33. St. Philip Vestry, 25 October 1819.

34. Ibid., 9 February 1808.

35. Colthurst Journal, see Chap. I, fn. 19, and illustration facing p. 65.

36. Burley, *Memorandum*.

37. Thorne and Kimball, *Emancipation*, p. 230.

38. *Liberal*, 6 March 1839.

39. CO 28/127, despatches 2 and 3 of 2 January 1839.
40. *Liberal,* 6 March 1839.

Chapter 6

1. *Barbadian,* 7 August 1841.
2. *Liberal,* 16 February 1859.
3. Davy, *West Indies,* pp. 66-67.
4. *Report of the Commission on Poor Relief 1875-1877* (Barbados, 1878). References to this report will in future be omitted from the notes where the source is mentioned in the text.
5. *Liberal,* 5 and 9 February 1859.
6. Christ Church Vestry, 28 March 1860.
7. Davy, *West Indies,* p. 65.
8. *Barbadian,* 7 August 1841.
9. *Barbados Agricultural Reporter,* 16 November 1875.
10. Davy, *West Indies,* p. 71.
11. *Minutes of Assembly* (1872-1873), app. A.
12. *Blue Book,* 1833.
13. Davy, *West Indies,* p. 68.
14. I am indebted to Mrs. Joycelin Massiah, for the use of her notes on the census results of the years 1851 to 1911.
15. *Appendices to the Report of the Poor Relief Commission: 1875-1879,* in the possession of Mr. Edward Stoute, of Barbados, who kindly made them available to me.
16. *Blue Book,* 1874.
17. Davy, *West Indies,* pp. 68-69.
18. *Barbados Globe,* 24 September 1838.
19. Schomburgk, *History,* pp. 84-85.
20. *Appendices to Poor Relief Report.*
21. Vaquero, *Life and Adventure in the West Indies* (London: Bale, Sons and Danielson, Ltd., 1914), p. 125; Hyatt Verrill, *Isles of Spice and Palm* (New York: D. Appleton & Co., 1915), pp. 161-162.
22. Davy, *West Indies,* p. 69.
23. Christ Church Vestry, 30 March 1857.
24. *Register of Proprietors of Copyright,* no. 34 of 13 February 1906.
25. Colthurst, *Journal.*
26. C. W. Day, *Five Years' Residence in the West Indies* (London, 1852), pp. 30-31.
27. *Barbadian,* 9 January 1836.
28. *Poor Relief Report.*
29. *Appendices to Poor Relief Report.*

30. Schomburgk, *History*, p. 196.
31. Greville John Chester, *Transatlantic Sketches*, (London, 1869), p. 100.
32. *Barbadian*, 7 August 1841; 14 July and 4 August 1847.
33. Original Act.
34. *Appendices to Poor Relief Report*.
35. Davy, *West Indies*, pp. 65-66.
36. Mrs. Flannigan, *Antigua and the Antiguans; a full account of the colony and its inhabitants*, vol. II (London, 1844), p. 100.
37. Lady Blake, "A Day in Barbados," in *Timehri*, IX (1895):69.
38. *Barbadian*, 13 May 1857; *Minutes of Assembly* (1872-1873), app. A.
39. George P. Paul, *Report on Ankylostomiasis Infection—Survey of Barbados* (New York: International Health Board, 1917), pp. 49-54.
40. John Davy, *Lectures on the study of chemistry ... and discourses on agriculture* (London, 1849), pp. 285-286.
41. *Barbadian*, 24 May and 25 June 1860.
42. *Minutes of Council and Assembly* (1875-1876), app. AAA.

Chapter 7

1. *Minutes of Assembly*, 13 July, 29 December 1847.
2. *Barbadian*, 27 July 1847.
3. James Pope-Hennessy, *Verandah* (London: Allen and Unwin, 1964), p. 181.
4. Burley, *Memorandum*.
5. Eliot, *Christianity and Slavery*, p. 226.
6. *Appendices to Poor Relief Report*.
7. St. James Vestry, 17 March 1879.
8. *Barbadian*, 22 September, 16 October 1841.
9. *Barbadian*, 7 March 1838; *Poor Relief Report*.
10. *Liberal*, 20 August 1842; *Barbadian*, 6 May 1857; Christ Church Vestry, 8 April 1875.
11. *Barbadian*, 7 March 1846.
12. Ibid., 14 January 1860.
13. *West Indian*, 27 February 1877.
14. St. John Vestry, 25 March 1840; *Minutes of Assembly*, 5 May 1896.
15. Laws of Barbados, 6 September 1887.
16. *Minutes of Assembly*, 3 December 1895.
17. *Minutes of Assembly*, 5 May 1896, Doc. 123.
18. *Official Gazette*, 19 November 1896.
19. *Barbadian*, 23 April 1836; 16 June 1838; 18 January 1840.
20. *Minutes of Assembly*, 20 August; 1, 15 October, 1850.
21. Ibid., 21 August 1869.
22. Ibid., 28 July 1875.

23. Ibid., 17 February 1880.
24. Laws of Barbados, 1880-1881.
25. *Blue Book*, 1838.
26. St. George Vestry, 19 August 1857.
27. *Blue Book*, 1839, 1843.
28. *Barbadian*, 18 April 1840.
29. *Annual Reports of the Barbados Society for the Education of the Poor in the Principles of the Established Church.*
30. "Journal of Captain William Bell," *BMHS Journal* XXX, no. 1, (November 1962): 32–33. The school for black and coloured children must have been St. Mary's, which had been established in 1818 on the initiative of the Governor, Lord Combermere.
31. Rolph, *Brief Account*, p. 44.
32. CO 318/138, West India Miscellany, Misc. 838, vol. 7.
33. Davy, *West Indies*, p. 69.
34. Laws of Barbados, 24 October 1850.
35. *Minutes of Assembly*, 28 September 1869.
36. E. T. Price, "Redlegs of Barbados," *BMHS Journal* XXIX, no. 2, (February 1962): p. 49; *West Indian*, 17 April 1885.
37. *Barbadian*, 25 August 1849.
38. St. George Vestry, 7 May 1849.
39. Shirley Gordon, *Century of West Indian Education* (London: Longmans, 1963), pp. 94-95.
40. A. G. Williams, "The Development of Education in Barbados 1834-1958" (unpublished MA thesis), provides valuable information on this aspect of the educational system.
41. *Minutes of Assembly*, 7 April 1846.
42. Laws of Barbados, 24 October 1850.
43. F. A. Hoyos, *Builders of Barbados* (London: Macmillan, 1972), p. 54.
44. Laws of Barbados, 21 December 1858.
45. *Minutes of Assembly*, 10 January 1860.
46. *Minutes of Assembly*, 26 February 1874.
47. Shirley Gordon, "Documents Which Have Guided Educational Policy In The West Indies—The Mitchinson Report, Barbados, 1875," *Caribbean Quarterly* IX, no. 3, (September 1963), provides a full evaluation.
48. *Minutes of Assembly*, 21 April, 5 June 1875 and appendices U, X.
49. Ibid., 14 November 1876.
50. *Official Gazette*, 16 November 1876.
51. Hoyos, *Builders*, p. 70.
52. *West Indian*, 29 September 1876.
53. *Minutes of Council*, 22 November 1876.
54. *West Indian*, 14 November 1876.
55. *West Indian*, 9, 12, 16 January 1877.
56. *Globe*, 4 October 1899.

57. *Minutes of Assembly,* 1877-1878, app. B.
58. Laws of Barbados, 9 December 1878.
59. *Blue Book,* 1878, 1881, 1882.
60. *Minutes of Council,* 7 October 1879.
61. Laws of Barbados, 19 March 1884.
62. *Blue Book,* 1880.
63. Christ Church Vestry, 25 October 1880.
64. St. Lucy Vestry, 11 February 1882.
65. *Minutes of Assembly,* 13 December 1892.
66. Laws of Barbados, 12 June 1894.
67. Laws of Barbados, 13 June 1894; R. V. Taylor, "The Butcher Trust and Golden Ridge Plantation," *BMHS Journal* XIX, no. 1, (November 1951): 4-5.
68. G. W. Roberts, "Emigration from Barbados," *Social and Economic Studies.* IV, no. 3, (September 1955) provides further details.
69. Laws of Barbados, 20 July 1836; 26 April 1839.
70. *Barbadian,* 30 March, 4 September 1839.
71. Laws of Barbados, 22 September 1840.
72. *Barbadian,* 13 July 1857.
73. Laws of Barbados, 23 March 1864; Roberts, "Emigration," p. 254.
74. Laws of Barbados, 10 September 1864.
75. *Minutes of Assembly,* 1872-1873, app. F.
76. *Barbadian,* 28 January 1860.
77. CO 28/129, Barbados despatch, 26 January 1859; Hincks' undated memorandum preceding Colonial Office despatch, 8 April 1859 in BDA In-despatches.
78. CO 260/92, St. Vincent despatch 64 of 11 July 1859.
79. CO 28/190, Jamaica despatch 992 of 25 August 1859.
80. Bahamas despatch 38, 25 April 1860.
81. CO 28/190, Grenada despatch 40, 8 August 1859.
82. *Minutes of Assembly,* 27 September 1859; 10 January 1860.
83. *Jamaica Standard,* 24 December 1859; *Trelawney Advertiser,* 8 March 1860.
84. *Minutes of Assembly,* 8 May 1860.
85. *Barbadian,* 18 May 1860.
86. Barbados despatch 12 March 1860.
87. Colonial Officer letter 52, 14 May 1860 enclosing Emigration Commissioner's letter, 27 April 1860.
88. *Minutes of Assembly,* 23 January, 19 February 1861.
89. *Barbadian,* 25 June 1860; 4 February 1861.
90. *Minutes of Assembly,* St. Vincent, 7 January 1862.
91. St. Vincent despatch, 18 February 1860.
92. *Appendices to Poor Relief Report.*
93. Colonial Secretary, St. Vincent, 22 August 1865.

94. Personal communication from Professor John E. Adam of the University of Minnesota.

95. Superintendent of Emigration, Third Report.

96. Based on analysis of information from St. George's Parish Registers.

97. Lands Registry, Grenada, deed of 10 February 1940 recording the leasing of the estate by Rosabelle Patterson to John Edward Elms.

98. M. G. Smith, *Stratification in Grenada* (Berkeley and Los Angeles: University of California Press, 1965), pp. 14-15.

99. Superintendent of Emigration, Reports for 1873-1877.

100. Laws of Barbados, 15 June 1881.

101. *Minutes of Assembly*, 31 December 1895.

102. William A. Paton, *Down the Islands, a Voyage to the Caribbee* (New York, 1887), p. 153.

103. *Official Gazette*, 17, 20, 24 May 1897.

104. *Minutes of Assembly*, 12 June 1900, Doc. 31.

105. CO 28/282, Washington despatches 325, 369 Commercial, 16 September, 10 November 1913.

106. Colonial Secretary, letter, 7 May 1900.

Chapter 8

1. George H. H. McLellan, *Some Phases of Barbadian Life—Tropical Scenes and Studies,* (Demarara: Argosy Co. Ltd., 1909), pp. 17-20.

2. A. Hyatt Verrill, *West Indies of Today* (New York: Dodd, Mead and Co., 1931), p. 142.

3. Frederick Treves, *Cradle of the Deep* (London: Smith, Elder and Co., 1908), pp. 41-42.

4. Verrill, *West Indies*, p. 142.

5. McLellan, *Phases*, pp. 17-20.

6. Verrill, *Isles of Spice and Palm*, pp. 161-162.

7. Treves, *Cradle*, pp. 41-42.

8. Author of *Cavaliers and Roundheads of Barbados*.

9. Davis Papers, Box 1, Env. 38. There seems, however, to be no trace of this correspondence among the Carnegie papers held by the Library of Congress.

10. *Barbados Agricultural Reporter*, 19 January 1915.

11. *Spectator*, 5 April 1913.

12. CO 28/281, Barbados Confidential despatch, 17 June 1913.

13. Census Report of 1911.

14. Census Reports of 1921 and 1946.

15. *Nation*, 17 February 1974.

16. CO 28/281, despatch of 17 June 1913, Enc. 3.
17. Harry Franck, *Roaming through the West Indies* (New York: Ribbon Books, 1920), p. 373.
18. E. T. Price, "The 'Redlegs' of Barbados," *BMHS Journal* XXIX, no. 2, (February 1962): p. 49.
19. Act of 21 November 1921.
20. *Minutes of Assembly*, 26 May 1914.
21. *Minutes of Assembly*, 16 September 1919; 5 June 1923.
22. CO despatch 128, 14 September 1923; *Minutes of Assembly*, 4 March 1924.
23. *Barbados Herald*, 9, 16 February; 15, 19 March; 5 April 1924.
24. *Minutes of Assembly*, 21 June 1925.
25. *Minutes of Assembly*, 23 April 1926; 16 August 1927, Doc. 9, 10. January 1928; 6 November 1928.
26. *Minutes of Assembly*, 28 October 1930; 19 July 1932.
27. By 1972, according to the *Annual Report of the Public Health Laboratory* for that year, only 2 out of 643 stools examined showed the presence of hookworm.
28. George Bernard, *Wayside Sketches—Pen Pictures of Barbadian Life* (Barbados: Advocate Press, 1934). This rather rare publication has an introduction by Clennell Wickham, sometime editor of the *Barbados Herald*, and was lent to me by his son, John Wickham. George Bernard is a pseudonym for Gordon Bell, school master and writer, well known for his article on "The Negro in Barbados" in Nancy Cunard's *Negro Anthology*.
29. CO 28/297, despatch 155, 18 June 1920.
30. *Advocate* of 13 November 1971 contains articles on the fiftieth anniversary of the firm. They provide much useful information on the Goddard family and also an assessment of its contribution not only to the economy but also to the society of Barbados.
31. Census Reports of 1911, 1921, 1946.
32. CO 28/281, despatch of 17 June 1913, Enc. 1.
33. Ibid.
34. See Chapter IV, note 3.
35. Records of Drax Hall, BDA 29/11/20.
36. CO 28/281, despatch 17 June 1913, Enc. 1.
37. Derek Bickerton, "The Redlegs of Barbados," *Sunday Advocate Magazine Section*, concluding article of series appearing from 28 May to 2 July 1961.
38. W. A. Beckles, *The Barbados Disturbances (1937)* (Barbados: Advocate Co. Ltd., 1937) and discussion with Mr. E. R. L. Ward, who was one of the members of the Commission of Enquiry.

Bibliography

Only works used extensively in this study are cited here; the notes provide a detailed guide to other relevant material available.

Manuscript Sources:

Barbados Public Library. Lucas Transcripts (Minutes of Council and Miscellaneous).

Boston Public Library. John Bowen Colthurst, *Journal as a special magistrate in the islands of Barbados and St. Vincent, July 1835-August 1838.*

British Museum. *Additional MSS. 11411 f. 9, 43507 ff. 1-5.*

              Egerton MSS. 2395 f. 602.

              King's Manuscripts. 205 ff. 456-473.

              Stowe MSS. 755 f. 19.

              Thomasson Tracts. 669 f. 11(115).

Public Record Office, London. Shaftesbury Papers. PRO 30/24/49.

Royal Commonwealth Society, London. Darnell N. Davis Papers.

Official Documents:

These are available in the Barbados Department of Archives except where stated otherwise.

Acts and Statutes of the Island of Barbados. John Jennings. London: 1654. (British Museum).

The Laws of Barbados. Richard Rawlin. London: 1699. (Barbados Museum and Historical Society).

Acts of Assembly passed in the Island of Barbados from 1648-1718. London: 1732. (Barbados Public Library).

Acts passed in the island of Barbados. From 1643 to 1762. Richard Hall.

London: 1764.

The Public Acts in Force: passed by the Legislature of Barbados, from May 11th 1762 to April 8th 1800, inclusive. Samuel Moore. London: 1801.

Public Acts in Force 1800-1845. In seven volumes, published in 1836, 1842, 1843, 1844 and 1845. (C.O. 30 in the Public Record Office, London, contains copies of laws passed between 1643 and 1843).

Barbados Blue Books

Calendar of State Papers, Colonial Series, America and the West Indies, 1574-1738.

Census Reports, 1715, 1851, 1861, 1871, 1881, 1891, 1911, 1921, 1946.

Despatches (C.O. 28 in the Public Record Office, London, contains the complete record; the material in the Barbados Department of Archives is limited).

Annual Reports of the Superintendent of Emigration, 1873-1877.

Minutes of Assembly, whether in transcript form or otherwise, from 1738 to 1818 and from 1838 to the present day. (Certain gaps can be filled by reference to C.O. 31 in the Public Record Office, London).

Vestry Minute Books. (Some of the early Vestry Minute Books for the Parish of St. John are available at the Barbados Museum and Historical Society).

Wills. Original Wills and Record Books.

Newspapers:

These are available in the Barbados Department of Archives except where stated otherwise.

Agricultural Reporter, 1870-1881, 1883-1899.

Barbadian, 1822-1861.

Barbados Gazette, 1787-1789.

Barbados Herald, 1880-1896.

Barbados Mercury, 1783-1784, 1787-1789.

Barbados Mercury and *Bridgetown Gazette,* 1805-1825, 1835, 1839, 1848.

Globe, 1886-1899 (1837-1838 and 1839-1841 in the P.R.O., C.O. 33).

Liberal, 1837-1859.

Weekly Herald, 1919-1931 (Barbados Public Library).

West Indian, 1876-1885.

Lists of Emigrants:

Hotten, J. C. *The Original Lists of Persons of Quality and Others who Emigrated to America.* London: 1874.

"Servants to Foreign Plantations from Bristol, England to Barbados 1654-1686." *Journal of the Barbados Museum and Historical Society,* 14 19.

A List of Emigrants from England to America 1682-1692. Transcribed by Michael Ghirelli. Baltimore: Magna Carta Book Co., 1968.

A List of Emigrants from England to America 1718-1759. Transcribed by Jack and Marion Kaminkov. Baltimore: Magna Carta Book Co., 1964.

Original Lists of Emigrants in Bondage from London to the American Colonies 1719-1744. Transcribed by Marion and Jack Kaminkov. Baltimore: Magna Carta Book Co., 1967.

"List of Prisoners of the '45 Rising." *Journal of the Barbados Museum and Historical Society* 30: 73-90.

Printed Works:

Bridenbaugh, Carl. *Vexed and Troubled Englishmen, 1590-1642.* Oxford: Clarendon Press, 1968.

Bridenbaugh, Carl and Roberta. *No Peace Beyond the Line: the English in the Caribbean, 1624-1690.* New York: Oxford University Press, 1972.

Burns, Sir Alan. *History of the West Indies.* 2d rev. ed. London: Allen and Unwin, 1965.

Davis, N. Darnell. *The Cavaliers and Roundheads of Barbados 1650-1652.* Georgetown, British Guiana, 1887.

Davy, John. *The West Indies before and since Slave Emancipation.* London: 1854.

Harlow, V. T. *A History of Barbados, 1625-1685.* Oxford: Clarendon Press, 1926. Reprinted New York: Negro Universities Press, 1969.

Ligon, Richard. *A True and Exact History of the Island of Barbados.* 1659, 1673. Reprinted London: Frank Cass, 1970.

Poyer, John. *The History of Barbados.* London: 1808. Reprinted London: Frank Cass, 1971.

Schomburgk, Robert H. *The History of Barbados.* London: 1848. Reprinted London: Frank Cass, 1971.

Smith, Abbott Emmerson. *Colonists in Bondage: White Servitude and Convict Labour in America, 1607-1776.* Chapel Hill: University of North Carolina Press, 1947.

Smith, Captain John. *The True Travels, Adventures, and Observations of Captaine John Smith in Europe, Asia, Africa and America, from Anno Domini 1593 to 1629.* London: 1630.

Sturge, Joseph, and Harvey, Thomas. *The West Indies in 1837.* London: Hamilton, Adams, 1838.

Thome, J. A., and Kimball, J. H. *Emancipation in the West Indies.* New York: Anti-Slavery Society, 1838.

Articles:

Bickerton, Derek. "The Redlegs of Barbados." *Sunday Advocate* (Magazine Section) 28 May-2 July 1961.

Price, E. T. "The Redlegs of Barbados." *Journal of the Barbados Museum and Historical Society,* 19: 47-52.

Stoute, Edward A. "The Poor Whites of Barbados." *The Bajan and South Caribbean.* November-December 1971, January-March 1972.

Index

The ISLAND of BARBADOES.

Divided into its Parishes,
with the Roads, Paths, &c.
According to an Actual and
Accurate Survey.

By H. Moll Geographer.

Explanation

- ⌕ Towns
- ⌂ Churches
- ▫ Fortifications
- ☷ Plantations of greatest Note or Sugar Works of three windmills
- ⋉ of two Mills
- · of one Mill
- . Plantations of less Note &c.
- ✕✕ Rocks under Water

Contents of the Parishes

Parish	Acres
Christ Church	14310
St. Philip	15040
St. Michael	9580
St. George	10795
St. John	8600
St. James	
St. Thomas	
St. Joseph	
St. Andrew	
St. Peter	8330
St. Lucy	8725

in all 106470

Which amounts to 166 Square miles, ye greatest length 21 miles, the greatest breadth 12 or 14 miles. Bridge Town ye Capital is a very Handsom well built Town, situated on a safe & commodious Bay, and very good Roads. See pag.g above 195 in S.E. from Jamaica. The nearest part of ye Continent to Barbadoes is Surinam, which lies about a day & a half Sail from it.

Barbadoes ye Chief of ye Caribbee Islands was discovered in ye Reign of King James ye 1st. The first settled about Bridge Town, & not being at ye same enriching rich, & the returns from thence very considerable, the settlements prospering in so flourishing a manner, that in ye Year 1676, when this Island was in its best Estate, there were 70,000 Europeans, & 80,000 Negroes upon it, which in proportion to the Land, was more populous than England.

Place names (map)

Consets
Conset
Congor Rock
Adamsons Bay
Culpeper Warren
The Rock three Boys
Tent Bay
St. Josephs River
Round Rock
Chalky
Scotland River
Pico Teneriffe
Gays Cove
Corbets Bay
The Land Lock
Cuckolds Pt.
Waits Bay
Jacobs Bay
Nans Bay
Kings Bay
Goat House Bay
River Bay
Lather Bay
Middle Bay
Creek Bay
Abbots Bay
Sandy hill
Gents Bay
Austs Bay
Gouldings
Strouds Pt.
Lambert Pt.
Strouds Bay
Norses Bay
Great Head
Maycock
Clinton
Harrison H. Row
Speights Town
Spring Head
The 4 Hills
Clarendon Fort
Margarets Bay
Roads Bay
Queen

St. ANDREWS P.
St. PETERS P.
St. LUCYS P.
St. LUCYS Church.
All Saints Chap.
St. IOS
Scotland